How the Japanese Learn to Work

The Nissan Institute/Routledge Japanese Studies Series

Editorial Board:

J.A.A. Stockwin, Nissan Professor of Modern Japanese Studies, University of Oxford and Director, Nissan Institute of Japanese Studies

Teigo Yoshida, formerly Professor of the University of Tokyo, and now Professor, The University of the Sacred Heart, Tokyo

Frank Langdon, Professor, Institute of International Relations, University of British Columbia, Canada

Alan Rix, Professor of Japanese, University of Queensland and currently President of the Japanese Studies Association of Australia

Junji Banno, Professor, Institute of Social Science, University of Tokyo

Other titles in the series:

The Myth of Japanese Uniqueness *Peter N. Dale*
The Emperor's Adviser: Saionji Kinmochi and pre-war Japanese politics *Lesley Connors*
Understanding Japanese Society *Joy Hendry*
Banking Policy in Japan: American attempts at reform during the occupation *William Minoru Tsutsui*

Forthcoming:

Japanese Religions *Brian Bocking*
Japan in World Politics *Reinhard Drifte*
A History of Economic Thought in Japan *Tessa Morris-Suzuki*
The Establishment of Constitutional Government in Japan *Junji Banno*
Japan's First Parliaments 1890–1910 *R.H.P. Mason, Andrew Fraser and Philip Mitchell*
Industrial Relations in Japan: The Peripheral Sector *Norma Chalmers*
Educational Reform in Contemporary Japan *Leonard Schoppa*

Militarization in Contemporary Japan *Glen Hook*
Japanese Economic Development in Theory and Practice *Penny Francks*
The Modernization of Written Japanese *Nanette Twine*
Japan and Protection *Javed Maswood*
Japan's Nuclear Development *Michael Donnelly*
The Soil, by Nagatsuka Takashi: A portrait of rural life in Meiji Japan *translated and introduced by Ann Waswo*

Biotechnology Policy in Japan *Malcolm Brock*

HOW THE JAPANESE LEARN TO WORK

Ronald P. Dore and Mari Sako

ROUTLEDGE
London and New York

First published in 1989 by
Routledge
11 New Fetter Lane, London EC4P 4EE
29 West 35th Street, New York NY 10001

Typeset by Mews Photosetting, Beckenham, Kent
Printed and bound in Great Britain by
Biddles Ltd, Guildford and King's Lynn

British Library Cataloguing in Publication Data

Dore, Ronald P., *1925–*
    How the Japanese learn to work.
    1. Japan. Vocational education
    I. Title II. Sako, Mari
    370.11'3'0952
    ISBN 0-415-03071-4

Library of Congress Cataloging in Publication Data

Dore, Ronald Philip.
        How the Japanese learn to work / Ronald P. Dore and Mari Sako.
            p. cm. — (The Nissan/Routledge Japanese studies series)
        Bibliography: p.
        Includes index.
        ISBN 0-415-03071-4
        1. Vocational education — Japan. 2. Occupational training — Japan.
    I. Sako, Mari. II. Title. III. Series.
    LC1047.J3D67   1989
    373.2'46'0952–dc19   89-5953
                                                                    CIP

This work was produced under contract with the Manpower Services
Commission. The views expressed are those of the authors and do not
necessarily reflect those of the MSC or any other government
department.

Contents

List of figures and tables

General Editor's Preface

Almost imperceptibly, during the 1980s, Japan has become 'hot news'. The successes of the Japanese economy and the resourcefulness of her people have long been appreciated abroad. What is new is an awareness of her increasing impact on the outside world. This tends to produce painful adjustment and uncomfortable reactions. It also often leads to stereotypes and arguments based on outdated or ill-informed ideas.

The Nissan Institute/Routledge Japanese Studies Series (previously the Nissan Institute/Croom Helm Japanese Studies Series) seeks to foster an informed and balanced — but not uncritical — understanding of Japan. One aim of the series is to show the depth and variety of Japanese institutions, practices and ideas. Another is, by using comparison, to see what lessons, positive and negative, can be drawn for other countries. There are many aspects of Japan which are little known outside that country but which deserve to be better understood.

Education is a field where the Japanese experience is attracting increasing interest, with evidence mounting of impressive performance in basic subjects in Japanese schools. In this book Professor Dore and Dr Sako investigate vocational training and its place in Japanese education and industry. Perhaps the most important lesson they draw is that in Japan real, not token, education is enjoyed by nearly the whole population, and not just by a meritocratic or wealthy elite. Because abilities and aspirations differ, not everybody is educated to the same level, but with a general atmosphere of respect for education the attainments of even the less able appear strikingly impressive. Moreover, there is a good mesh between the school and the workplace, for reasons which sometimes seem surprising. Not all aspects of Japanese educational practice need be regarded as admirable and the system has many critics within Japan. Nevertheless, the fact that Japanese education produces a largely rational and employable population is surely a merit which deserves to be treated with the utmost seriousness.

J.A.A. Stockwin
Director, Nissan Institute of Japanese Studies,
University of Oxford

Preface

In the early 1870s a delegation of senior Japanese statesmen spent nearly a year touring, and studying, the United States and Britain. They visited centres of government, of commerce and, in Britain especially, of industry. The recently republished record of that visit (Kume 1978) with its detailed sketches and descriptions of industrial processes, contained numerous reflections on what it was that made Britain and America so prosperous while Japan remained so poor. It was not so much, the delegation concluded, in industriousness that the difference lay, nor in natural resources. It lay rather in the application of science to production, in planning, organization and disciplined skill.

The delegation's return confirmed the conviction of Japan's leaders that the road to a secure and respected place in the international system lay in a national endeavour to 'catch up' in the accumulation of industrial skills as much as in the accumulation of industrial capital, that Japan was at the beginning of a long apprenticeship. One of the first tasks of their ambassador in London was to recruit a group of young Scotsmen to found the first Tokyo college of engineering.

And cultural lags are such that only in recent years have these perceptions begun to change. The manifest reversal in their rankings in industrial power is only now just beginning to make the Japanese more, as it makes the British less, complacent. But still, as Chapter 6 suggests in some detail, a Japanese factory is more likely than a British factory to be a learning organization. The ruling assumption is more likely to be: 'We've still got a long way to go to reach satisfactory levels' rather than 'We're doing pretty well'. A recurring need for special training programmes is taken for granted. They do not have to be justified on the grounds that 'these boffins keep coming up with something new and we jolly well need to keep up', but are perfectly acceptable even when they are presented as getting people up to long-established levels of satisfactory competence.

And what has certainly not changed is the assumption, which grew quite naturally out of that century-long preoccupation with Japan's backwardness, that the state has a vital role to play in raising the nation's standards of vocational competence.

In the standard theory of liberal democracy, the state's involvement in vocational training is justified only on the grounds of market failure. Training has a lot of external economies which you cannot, except through taxation and collective public action, get the beneficiaries to pay for — the benefits nurses get from having doctors to work with, the benefits employers get from having sick employees cured, the benefits we all get from having competent soldiers to defend us, etc. Hence, although we can still rely to some extent on the market to provide individuals with what they want — i.e. opportunities to develop the talents they need to sell in the market in order to get the income they desire — the market needs a lot of supplementation by the state.

Of course, that argument from individual interests has never, anywhere, been a complete account of the reasons why liberal democracies have interested themselves in vocational training. National considerations — to strengthen 'national champion' firms against their foreign rivals, to raise the nation's strategic power — have been powerful concerns in Britain ever since alarm at Germany's industrial strength began to grow at the turn of the century. But still, in so far as one can measure the balance in such matters, individualistic arguments about opportunities for self-development have tended to dominate in Britain.

But hardly so in Japan. For the last hundred years, the national need to build up skills has been part of a collective national drive to strengthen Japan's international position. At first it was a matter of national survival. That assured — by the time the delegation returned in 1872 — the objective became to make the country strong enough, in the first instance, to persuade foreigners to amend the 'unequal treaties' which they forced on Japan in the 1850s, a quarter-century struggle still well remembered today, and the subject, not surprisingly, of a multi-billion yen movie in 1986.

Japan's international position today, and her ranking in the various pecking orders of international competition, are beyond all except the wilder dreams of the Japanese of the 1880s — or of the 1950s, for that matter. But still, old assumptions and old motivation patterns persist. After a century striving to be accepted as an equal, the inertia of the striving reflex sets new goals — to become first among equals. Hence the journalistic popularity of newspaper polls about Japan's standing — is she ahead, behind or level with the US in cell fusion techniques, in laser semiconductors? How does Japan compare with Germany in the development of new operatic forms?

Hence the assumptions about the role of the state in vocational training which have shaped Japan's current VET institutions over the last century remain largely unchanged, even if a lot of their manifestations today smack more of bureaucratic nannying than of leadership in a concerted drive for success. This circumstance will be reflected in many of the succeeding chapters — in what is said about the guiding philosophy of the general education system, and especially apropos of the state's role in setting standards of vocational competence which will be described in Chapter 7.

The other thing about Japanese society which powerfully shapes the system to be described — another product of history and culture — is the kind of *moral* feelings the Japanese have about needing to be good at their jobs. Whether because of the efforts of state agencies to preach the national need for competence over the last century or for some other reason, the Japanese do tend to feel that competence is a moral duty and not just a means of earning money by giving satisfaction, that sloppiness is a sin and not just something to avoid because it puts you in danger of getting the sack.

That also counts for something. It is a factor in the response which private firms show to government initiatives, and in the initiatives they take without prompting. It is a factor in the response of the individual workers to enterprise programmes. It is a factor, too, in the vigour of the private enterprise training sector described in Chapter 5.

But the important role played by these cultural factors in shaping the Japanese vocational education and training (hereafter VET) system does not mean that there are no lessons to be learned from it. There may well be, to begin with, hints to be found in individual institutional devices for financing training and motivating take-up. There seems, also, to be a good deal which might be learned from nuts-and-bolts pedagogical practices in Japan, though on that we have very little to say in this book.

What we hope we do show however, is a different way in which one can learn by examining Japan. Confrontation with a system built on assumptions somewhat different from our own brings those assumptions into relief. It causes us to question ideas which we might otherwise never question, and to think of possible alternatives we might never have thought of — of solutions, one might even say, to problems we never realised we had.

COMMON ASSUMPTIONS ABOUT VOCATIONAL TRAINING WHICH JAPAN BRINGS INTO QUESTION

Here, for example, is a list of some of the assumptions which are often — not universally, to be sure, but often — implicit in the VET

xi

· policies and the VET policy debate in Britain and North America, assumptions the validity of which the example of Japan undoubtedly calls into question.

(i) That the most important thing is to get the most talented people well trained.

No country is more conscious of scarcity factors in the pool of talent than Japan. Yet its real comparative advantage seems to lie in the high attainment levels of its middle mass of workers at intermediate skill levels. The most striking British-Japanese difference in three-Rs attainments is among those in the bottom half of the ability range.

(ii) That industry must use its board and council memberships to influence the school and higher education system to be more responsive to industry's needs.

The school and university system under the aegis of the Japanese Ministry of Education keeps industry very much at arm's length. Vocational high schools and engineering faculties have fewer links with industry than their counterparts in this country. Engineering research is further towards the 'basic' as opposed to the 'applied'/ 'developmental' end of the spectrum in Japan than in Britain. The countervailing factors are (a) the performance of the school system in providing mastery of the basics, (b) the acceptance by employers that the responsibility for detailed job-oriented training is theirs, (c) the heavy involvement (in quite arduous quasi-voluntary leg-work) of private industry engineers in devising curricula and setting standards for the skill tests operated by ministries other than that of Education — MITI, the Ministries of Labour, Construction, Health and Welfare, Communications, Transport, etc. These exercise a powerful influence on all post-employment training.

(iii) That training is best provided by specialists in training.

Japanese firms rely relatively less on courses provided by training firms or outside consultants, more on mutual teaching, off-the-job as well as on but more often the latter, within the firm.

(iv) That expenditure on off-the-job training is a good measure of the extent to which a firm is a 'learning organization'.

Apart from the mutual teaching/on-the-job training just mentioned, Japanese emplóyees get a good deal of their training inexpensively through correspondence courses — of a traditional (pedagogically low-tech) kind.

(v) That vocational qualifications primarily tell one what their possessors have learned.

No-one really believes that Volkswagen employs German youths coming out of a bakery apprenticeship because they have acquired some transferable skills in measuring quantities and mixing ingredients which might come in handy in the paint shop. Yet discussions of VET often proceed as if that were the case. In fact, in any society, qualifications, especially at lower and intermediate levels, are often read largely, even primarily, as indicators of personality factors — application and willingness to 'fit in' — and of general learning ability. The transparency of this use of the vocational qualifications delivered in the general school system in Japan (vocational high schools and engineering faculties) — the transparency due to the commercial mock test and standarized score (*hensachi*) system and the high quality of research into recruitment processes in Japan — prompts one to look harder at these aspects in other countries too. Most people would acknowledge in principle that courses do get ability-labelled by received impressions of the 'calibre' of the students who get on them. They would acknowledge that this label affects (i) student motivation, (ii) pedagogical effectiveness, (iii) the likelihood that employers will offer graduates the jobs for which they have been trained, and (iv) their effectiveness in those jobs if they get them, and that effects in each of those dimensions feed back on the others. These considerations do surface in our debates, but always covertly. The anybody-can-be-taught-anything-provided-the-teacher's-good-enough ethos of the training industry all too often dominates — in Britain, for instance, in discussions of Training Workshops for the unemployed and of the Youth Training Scheme. In Japan the transparency of the screening functions of some vocational courses (vocational high schools) and the absence of screening functions in others (nationally tested vocational skill training) highlights the crucial importance of those screening functions which VET planners ignore at their peril.

(vi) That the state has a role in testing and certifying occupational competence only where public health and safety are involved or, possibly, in order to improve the working of the labour market.

Japanese Ministries are active in testing for the additional purpose of raising standards of competence — of plumbers and printers, cooks and computer-programmers — in the interests of national efficiency.

(vii) That the definition, testing and certification of occupational standards is best left either to self-regulating bodies of practitioners, or to the training institutions.

Japan acts more often on the assumption that only the customers have an unalloyed interest in maintaining high standards — the customers represented most often by the state; sometimes (as with welding) by the employers of the people they certify.

(ix) That the certifying of occupational competence is primarily a matter of certifying whole-package occupational roles: i.e., licences to practise — as a plumber, as a systems engineer, as a craftsman fitter, as a dentist.

While Japan also has a wide range of 'whole role' qualifications (state examinations for doctors, midwives, architects, etc.) this is very widely supplemented by what one might call the boy-scout-badge approach — the certifying, particularly at lower and intermediate skill levels, of discrete isolable skills, like the ability to drive a heavy goods vehicle, or to handle certain types of dangerous chemicals, or to use a turret lathe, or to install jacuzzi baths. The substantive content of these certification packages is determined by the logic of the job function. There is no need to fit it into a system of 'modules' or 'credits' with each credit guaranteed to represent X contact hours and Y credits adding up to the qualification of Master-Whumpfer. This results in less padding or skimping of training content, more functionally defined training, more flexibility in individual combinations of skills, and an easier linking of pay to performance rather than to some conventionally defined 'skill status'.

COMPETITIVENESS, THE VET RETHINK AND GERBIL

It is not hard to imagine a certain kind of response to all that — and one from which one cannot withhold a certain sympathy. 'OK. We see all that. Those are just the sort of points which would be made by people like you who have been seduced by this insidious Japanese tendency to see all matters in terms of national interest and efficiency, and not at all in terms of individual self-fulfillment, of providing the bases for individual competence and a sense of self-efficacy. And didn't you yourselves start off this introduction by explaining why Japan came to be so special in regard to competitiveness?'

True. We did. But the fact is that Japan is becoming less and less notable in these terms (and anyway never was so exceptional to anything like the same degree compared with the French or the Germans). The 'competitiveness imperative' began to hit Britain as its manufacturing import bill started to soar in the 1970s. In the US, it became the subject of Congressional cries of pain and Presidential commissions of inquiry in the early 1980s. Its most interesting manifestation in Britain is the 1987 Great Educational Reform Bill (or GERBIL).

That bill, the most radical piece of educational legislation since 1944, is a curious mixture. On the one hand it reflects the Thatcher radical doctrines of deregulation, individualism, free market choice and the whittling down of the state. Parent-consumers are going to be able to take charge of their local schools and, if they wish, take them out of the state system. But whereas the government seems to believe that deregulation of the buses, consumer choice and free competition will produce efficient local transport, the courage of its marketist beliefs fails when it comes to education. It manifestly does not believe that parental choice alone is going to produce schools which actually make children able to count, read and write. It is instead imposing, for the first time in British educational history, a state-prescribed core curriculum and state-prescribed standards of competence in numeracy and literacy which all children will be expected to attain.

There could be no clearer admission of the fact that, given the intensification of international competition which the cheapening of transport and communication has brought to the capitalist parts of the globe, states — even under Thatcherite, Friedmanite, Hayekian governments — can no longer opt out. They can no longer leave to the market the business of making their citizens economically efficient. Since our states, too, are being forced into the business the Japanese state has been more whole-heartedly engaged in for the last century, it behoves us to give rather careful thought to the solutions they have arrived at.

THE PLAN OF THE BOOK

These are the thoughts which have determined the emphases of the book which follows.

We begin with the general education system and stress not just the sheer quantity and intellectual quality of what goes on there, but also the moral quality and prestige status of the teaching and learning process, reflected as it is in the status and pay of teachers.

Chapter 2 is about who goes where — about the all-important screening processes within the system which determine which children, of what ability levels, are channelled into what types of school and why employers have very different expectations of a vocational school in a rural area and of a school with identical curriculum, staff and equipment in a big city.

The next three chapters give the factual picture of the three main types of institutional vocational training; the vocational high schools and vocational faculties of colleges and universities within the system supervised by the Ministry of Education; the public vocational schools under other Ministries and local governments; and the wide range of private vocational training schools, mostly offering one- or two-year courses for 18-year-old high-school leavers. At both the high school and the university level, explicitly vocational courses absorb about a third of the students. The courses tend to be wide-ranging and comprehensive rather than specialized — the assumption being that one is laying the basis for further learning rather than producing a complete product. The other two types of school provide more specialist courses; the private sector being numerically the most important (absorbing about one-fifth of high-school graduates), but of uneven quality.

Training within industry is the subject of the longest chapter, Chapter 6. The practices of Japanese firms cannot be understood, of course, except in the context of Japanese 'lifetime employment' practices but it is not by virtue of large budgets devoted explicitly to training that Japanese firms are differentiated from British or North American firms. They are 'learning organizations' because of the high level of mutual teaching-learning which goes on — partly pre-programmed in initial training periods, partly arising out of the introduction of new processes and products. It is partly self-directed by employees and there is a flourishing correspondence course industry (using quite traditional methods) which serves it. A lot depends on attitudes — the modest acceptance that everyone has much to learn, the acceptance by all supervisors that teaching is a part of every supervisory role. Those attitudes, in turn, are much dependent on the social characteristics of Japanese enterprises which, as compared with enterprises in Anglo-Saxon countries, are rather more like communities and rather less like markets where one sells the minimum effort for the maximum gain.

The qualification system and the vocational skill testing system are treated in some detail in Chapter 7. We show the extensive nature of the system, and elaborate some of the points made above — especially the Consumer Association/abuse of monopoly point about who validates standards (the practitioners or the trainers or the independent representatives of the customers) and the packaging point ('whole role' diplomas or 'boy scout badge' certificates) — the latter, of course, having a lot to do with pay systems which are steadily changing in Britain in a Japanese direction without a comparable change in training standards.

The last three chapters are about the policy superstructure. Chapter 8 gives details of financing and attempts the unusual task of an overall assessment of who (state, enterprise or individual household) finances how much of the national VET effort. It includes both the expenditures which normally enter into GNP calculations (like the salaries of trainers in both public and private sectors) and those which do not (like individuals' many hours of home study) and should at least prompt some reflection about the importance of the latter.

The last chapter briefly describes recent policy trends — if anything reinforcing existing patterns — and the penultimate describes the fragmented and uncoordinated nature of Japan's policy-making process. Rampant sectionalism and inter-ministerial rivalry are the price one pays for the energy and dedication which Japanese civil servants display in perfecting their own department's programmes.

That is only one of the trade-offs which the book outlines. There are few simple solutions in the VET business.

NOTE

For all illustrations of costs the yen has been translated into pounds at the rate £1 = ¥220.

Acknowledgements

The authors wish gratefully to acknowledge the help they have received from Kevin McCormick on the training of engineers, and also from their friends and mentors in Japan, among whom they would especially, if inevitably invidiously, pick out for mention: Aiwa Akagi, Ikuo Amano, Hideo Iwaki, Atusyoshi Ohe, Kazuhiko Otsuki and Kenji Tsunekawa.

1

The general school system

Much has been written about the contribution to Japan's economic efficiency of its general school system — the so-called 6–3–3–4 system under the control of the Ministry of Education, comprising:

- Kindergarten, which now enrols most 5-year-olds and well over a third of the 4-year-olds too.
- Primary schools (6–12) and middle schools (12–15) of the compulsory education age span.
- High schools (15–18), both general and vocational, which enrol about 95 per cent of the age group in their first year and graduate about 90 per cent.
- Two-year colleges (18–20) and four-year universities (18–22), with both vocationally specific and vocationally unspecific courses, which enrol nearly 40 per cent of the age group in their first years and graduate over nine-tenths of them.
- Five-year (15–20) Colleges of Technology with about two per cent of the age group.

Japan is well known for having what is probably in the younger age groups the world's best educated (at least most educated) population. The rapid expansion of the system and the, by international standards, very high enrolment levels in secondary and higher education, are clear enough from Table 1.1 showing the change over thirty years in the educational experience of new labour force entrants in manufacturing and finance. Let us begin by listing some of the other main characteristics of the system, besides its quantitative diffusion.

It is maintained at relatively low public cost — absorbing approximately 16 per cent of government expenditure (8.5 per cent of central; 23 per cent of local), but out of a total public expenditure budget well

1

Table 1.1 Educational composition of intake in selected industries, 1955-85

Manufacturing graduates	1955	1965	1975	1985
Middle School (15+)	264 (72)	387 (55)	49 (15)	—
High School (18+)	86 (23)	255 (36)	184 (57)	225 (65)
Technical College (20+)	—	0 (0)	4 (1)	4 (1)
College (20+)	2 (1)	9 (1)	20 (6)	30 (9)
University B.A. (22+)	16 (4)	49 (7)	62 (19)	81 (23)
Science, Engineering			34 (11)	44 (13)
Arts, Social Sciences			28 (9)	37 (11)
University M.A. (24+)	—	1 (0)	4 (1)	8 (2)
University PhD. (26+)	—	—	0.2	0.3
Total	368 (100)	701 (100)	323 (100)	348 (100)

Banking, Finance, Insurance, and Real Estate graduates	1955	1965	1975	1985
Middle School (15+)	2 (7)	1 (1)	—	—
High School (18+)	21 (72)	65 (82)	69 (62)	28 (37)
College (20+)	1 (3)	3 (4)	15 (13)	21 (28)
University (22+)	5 (17)	10 (13)	28 (25)	26 (35)
Total	29 (100)	79 (100)	112 (100)	75 (100)

Source: Nihon Recruit Centre, *Shinki-gakusotsu-sha saiyo tokei benran* (Collected statistics on recruitment of school and college leavers), 1986

under 20 per cent of GNP. Pupils and their families provide one-fifth of the 6.9 per cent of GNP which is estimated to be spent on the mainline school system. Much, but not all of that private expenditure is incurred in that segment of the system which is run — to central government specifications regarding minimal facilities and curriculum content — as a private business, either for profit (many of the high schools) or by non-profit trusts (some of the century-old universities, for example). The private four-year universities which enroll 70 per cent of all university students have received subsidies over the last decade which have brought their fees closer to, but still a long way above, those of national and public universities. The nearly thirty per cent of high school students in private schools pay in fees a rather higher proportion of the economic cost of their education, however. At the middle school level (3 per cent of pupils) and primary level (half of one per cent), private schools are of lesser numerical significance, though at least half of the middle school 3 per cent does represent a highly selected elite on track for the best universities.

Generally, the private sector divides into elite schools such as those just mentioned with highly competitive entrance examinations, and spill-over schools for those who cannot get into good public schools — or only into very low-prestige public schools. The bulk of the private universities are in the spill-over category.

All post-compulsory educational institutions have entrance examinations, and strict meritocratic rationing — among those who can afford the fees — is a universal and rigorously applied principle in both the public and the private sector (except for the lower reaches of the spill-over university hierarchy where donations can compensate for low marks). If the top university has 3,000 places, the top 3,000 scorers in the entrance examination, and only they, are admitted. A national achievement scale rating (like the American SAT) has been developed which admits of little unclarity as to which is the top university (for any particular subject) and which is each prefecture's top high school, and where, approximately, in the pecking order all the other universities and schools come.

Since employers take the topness or otherwise of universities and schools very much into account when recruiting (top firms take only from top universities), and since the bias towards lifetime employment means that initial recruitment is recruitment for careers, not just first jobs, a great deal is at stake in the educational competition. It is not just that the top prizes glitter. The prizes available to those who can get themselves rated in the third decile of the ability range glitter more than the prizes offered to those in the fourth. This, plus

3

Confucian educational traditions, accounts for the very high levels of expenditure of effort on the part of pupils, and of cash on the part of their parents.

It also accounts for the concentration of effort on basic subjects: Japanese language, maths and English — the staple subjects of the entrance examinations at both of the selection points — 15-plus and 18-plus. (See Tables 1.2 and 1.3 for curriculum structures.)

Table 1.2 Primary school timetable

Subjects	Year 1	2	3	4	5	6
Japanese language	272	280	280	280	210	210
Social Studies	68	70	105	105	105	105
Arithmetic	136	175	175	175	175	175
	(16%)	(19.2%)	(19.9%)	(17.2%)	(17.2%)	(17.2%)
Science	68	70	105	105	105	105
Music	68	70	70	70	70	70
Drawing & Craft	68	70	70	70	70	70
Domestic Science	—	—	—	—	70	70
PE	102	105	105	105	105	105
Moral education	34	35	35	35	35	35
Special activities	34	35	35	70	70	70
Total number of school hours	850	910	980	1,015	1,015	1,015

Source: Ministry of Education, 1982 Course of Study: Primary schools
N.B. One unit hour is 45 minutes.

It accounts, also, for the general acceptance of rigid uniformity of curriculum up to the end of high school — identity of content in the basic subjects and a minimal range of optional subjects. The constantly-heard demand for greater pupil choice, scope for teacher creativity, etc., always founders on the need to 'level the playing field' — to make sure that everybody has the same chance in the entrance competitions which determine life-chances.

Parents can, however, buy extra chances. And surveys suggest that, in the years before crucial examinations something like a half of city parents do — through an extensive network of private cram schools. They offer supplementation of school education with after-school and Sunday classes in the basic subjects — supplementation which, their parents hope, will notch up a child's rating by a crucial few extra points. The schools tend to be clearly differentiated into 'catch-up' and 'keep-up' classes for the less bright children whose parents are

worried about their falling behind in class, and high-flyer classes —
with tough entrance tests — for children aiming at some of the most
selective middle or high schools.

Table 1.3 Junior secondary school timetable

Subjects	Year 1	Year 2	Year 3
Japanese language	175	140	140
Social studies	140	140	105
Mathematics	105	140	140
	(10%)	(13.3%)	(13.3%)
Science	105	105	140
Music	70	70	35
Art	70	70	35
PE	105	105	105
Home Economics/Technology	70	70	105
Moral education	35	35	35
Special activities	70	70	70
Foreign language	105	105	140
Total number of school hours	1,050	1,050	1,050

Source: Ministry of Education. 1982 Course of Study: Middle Schools
N.B. One unit hour is 50 minutes.

Not all the out-of-school private extra classes are cram classes,
however. There are also music classes, calligraphy classes, foreign
language classes, abacus classes. They are proof that older Confucian traditions — the belief that self-development, self-cultivation are
desirable in themselves and a condition for citizen self-respect — also
have their force today.

Those two forces — the competitive drive to improve life chances
and the Confucian traditions — make acceptable a very high intensity
of schooling. Japanese children attend school for more hours a day,
for more days a week, for more weeks a year, than British children.
(See Tables 1.2 and 1.3.) In twelve years of schooling a Japanese
child gets as many classroom hours as a British child would get in
fourteen. Homework starts at the age of 7 or 8.

Schools are well-equipped (though not with computers, and
although the Japanese are by no means immune to the attractions of
snappy slogans with a vague high-tech aura, the phrase 'computer
literacy' appears to have no Japanese equivalent). Classes are large:
many in primary school contain over forty pupils, and high school

5

classes are no smaller; in private schools often larger. There are few discipline problems; the innocent co-operativeness of children in British primary schools seems in Japan to extend to the age of 8 — less innocent and more calculated, perhaps, at that age, but still co-operativeness. Bullying and physical violence in schools — not high schools where violence is concentrated in the US, but for the most part in the last year of middle school where the tensions of the selection system are concentrated — has recently become a matter of national concern; it has been front page news and one of the main reasons cited by the government for establishing the grand Ad Hoc Educational Reform Commission. The actual number of recorded incidents turns out to be minute compared with the size of the system. The fuss is a measure of the fact that the modal school is a rather gentle place.

They are relatively gentle places because, paradoxically, they are not particularly competitive places. It is not uncommon, to be sure, to post class lists showing who is top and who is bottom of the class. But that internal use of the stimulus of competition is not directly related to the really intense competition which is competition in the external market place, not in the classroom. One's direct rivals are strangers from other schools seeking entrance to the same next-level school, not one's classmates — to all of whom, without contradiction and in all sincerity, one could wish the same success as oneself.

Teachers work hard to sustain a co-operative, comradely, mutually helping atmosphere, and they have to work very hard at it indeed since streaming does not begin until high school entrance examinations stream 15-year-olds by school. There is no streaming in the compulsory education age span, and the maths curriculum which confronts the teachers of mixed-ability classes of 15-year-olds is closer to O-level than CSE standards. Much effort is expended, while gearing the pace of teaching to the average child, to feed extra material to the quick learners, and to give extra help to the slower learners.

One consequence of this is visible in the international studies of academic attainment in, for example, mathematics. Not only are average scores higher in Japan than in Britain; the dispersal around the average is also less. The most able British children do as well as the most able Japanese children; it is those in the lower half of the ability range who do so much better in Japan. It is a matter for speculation whether this is because, in Japan, they actually get more attention, or because the attention they do get is less likely to alienate them, or because of a greater cultural homogeneity in family circumstances in Japan or whether, indeed, historical patterns of marriage and mobility have produced a more genetically homogeneous population in Japan than in Britain.

Alienation worries everyone, if it happens. Children at the more individualistic end of the Japanese personality spectrum learn how difficult life is for those not spiritually integrated into the group. Japanese schools provide lessons not only in the horrors of isolation, but also in the inadmissible cruelty of letting others feel isolated. This training in groupishness is reinforced by, for example, the total absence of cleaning staff, the fact that it is the children's responsibility to clean 'our' classroom and 'our' school playground — a practice designed to inculcate, also, a sense of responsibility for one's environment, as well as drawing on older traditions which emphasize cleanliness, the dignity of manual work and the dangers of pride.

Although there is a general opinion that the quality of recruits into the teaching profession is declining, teachers remain well-respected and well-paid. If, to take the 1985 figures, the average salary for a teacher with 15–20 years' service (an average almost identical for primary/middle and for high school teachers) is set at 100, the average policeman with the same length of service earns 88 and the average pay of members of the Self-Defence Forces (all ranks, all ages) is 84. University graduates start at ¥190,400 in primary and middle schools, ¥188,700 in universities, and ¥159,170 in the Tokyo metropolitan police (1986 rates).

Teachers work hard for their money, out of school hours as well as in. In spite of the militancy of the main teachers' union which has conducted quite tough campaigns on matters such as the revival of militarism in history textbooks, there has never been a clear majority in the union for a stance of overt arm's-length contractualism. (The debate is conducted in the Confucian terms: 'Is teaching a form of intellectual labour or a *seishoku* a "calling" — literally "a holy profession"?') The 'calling' type of dedication is especially required of those in charge of final-year classes. For each of forty children in his 'home room class', for instance, a middle-school third-year teacher might well hold at least three *sansha-kon* (parent-teacher-child 'three-party consultations') about the child's future — which high school he would be best advised to apply for. And at least one of those sessions is likely to be in the child's home.

The curriculum remains a broad one until the end of high school. (See Table 1.4.) Every pupil, even in vocational schools, continues to study maths, Japanese literature, English, history, and general science. It is still almost as broadly based in the first two, general education, years of the university course. Real specialization begins only in the last two years of university. University teaching does tend to be school-like in its reliance on bucket theories of pedagogy —

Table 1.4 Senior high school course timetables

a. Credit requirements for students who wish to advance to arts departments
   of universities

Subject areas	Subjects	Grade 10th	Grade 11th	Grade 12th	Total credits
Japanese Language	Japanese Language I	5			5
	Japanese Language II		5		5
	Modern Japanese Language			3	3
	Classics			3	3
Social Studies	Contemporary Society	4			4
	Japanese History				
	World History		6*	4**	10
	Geography		(3x2)	(2x2)	
	Politics and Economy			2	2
Mathematics	Mathematics I	5			5
	Algebra & Geometry		3	2	5
	Basic Analysis		2	2	4
Science	Science I	4			4
	Science II			2	2
	Chemistry		} 3	} 2	} 5
	Biology				
Health and Physical Education	Physical Education	2	2	3	7
	Health	1	1		2
Art	Music I				
	Fine Arts I	} 2	} 1		} 3
	Calligraphy I				
Foreign Language	English I	5			5
	English II		2	3	5
	English II B		3		3
	English II C			4	4
Home Economics	General Home Economics	2	2		4
Additional credits		2	2	2	6
Total for all subjects		32	32	32	96
Homeroom activities		1	1	1	3
Club activities		1	1	1	3
GRAND TOTAL		34	34	34	102

* Six credits from two subjects from among Japanese History, World History
   and Geography (three credits for each subject).
**Four credits in two subjects from among Japanese History, World History
   and Geography (two credits for each subject).

b. Credit requirements for students who wish to advance to science departments
   of universities

Subject areas	Subjects	Grade 10th	Grade 11th	Grade 12th	Total credits
Japanese Language	Japanese Language I	5			5
	Japanese Language II		4		4
	Modern Japanese Language			4	4
Social Studies	Contemporary Society	4			4
	Japanese History	} 3	} 3	} 2	} 5
	Geography				
	Politics and Economy			2	2
Mathematics	Mathematics I	5			5
	Algebra & Geometry		3	2	5
	Basic Analysis		3	2	5
	Differential and Integral Calculus			3	3
Science	Science I	4			4
	Physics		3	3	6
	Chemistry		3	3	6
Health and Physical Education	Physical Education	2	2	3	7
	Health	1	1		2
Art	Music I	} 2	} 1		} 3
	Fine Arts I				
	Calligraphy I				
Foreign Language	English I	5			5
	English II		2	3	5
	English II B		3		3
	English II C			3	3
Home Economics	General Home Economics	2	2		4
Additional credits		2	2	2	6
Total for all subjects		32	32	32	96
Homeroom activities		1	1	1	3
Club activities		1	1	1	3
GRAND TOTAL		34	34	34	102

Source: National Institute of Educational Research, *Basic Facts and Figures about the Educational System in Japan, December 1983*

the student as receptacle into which knowledge and ideas have to be poured — though a lot of the pouring has to be done by the student himself, sitting down with his books in private study. Self-reliance and initiative-taking are required — less so stimulation of the critical and imaginative faculties which usually does not come until in his final year the student enters the *zemi* (the personal seminar group) of his chosen professor — and then only if he is lucky in his choice of professor.

So what may one conclude about the relation of this system to vocational preparation, to subsequent occupational performance and, by extension, to the efficiency of the national economy?

The high levels of effort input — across the board — produce high average — and minimal — levels of achievement in basic numeracy. This provides a good base for subsequent technical training, as well as, perhaps, contributing to the general respect for rationality in Japanese life (relative to, say, strength of character), and to the fact that wage discussions can proceed on the assumption that every worker understands how instantly to translate nominal wages into real wage terms.

High levels of effort also lead to a very high average level of fluency in the use of the written language, leading to a greater use of the recorded written word in industrial operations and business negotiations (to be distinguished from adherence to the letter of contract) than is usual in other societies.

These high average levels — a point recently stressed by Prais (1987) — involve a relatively small dispersal of achievement levels around the mean (relative to Britain, that is, if less so to Germany). The efforts expended on the slower learners in unstreamed middle schools, supplemented by extra lessons in cram schools for some, pay off in more than usually high levels of achievement for those around and below average.

Long school days and long school weeks, inurement to the requirement for unrelenting effort, the concentration of a lot of that effort in unsupervised homework, must help to produce people who can stick at correspondence courses, and do not feel resentfully deprived when they have to give up a number of Sundays to a skill training course.

Whether it enhances the capacity to enjoy life is a different matter. School serves, rather, to teach the classic Protestant ethical doctrine that life is primarily about fulfilling one's assigned duties and meeting deadlines and only secondarily about happiness or enjoyment. It teaches, too, the pleasures of achievement, and the dangers of resting on laurels and not recognizing the challenge of even greater possible

10

achievements. But it also teaches the need to choose one's challenges realistically — to know one's place, roughly, in the spectrum, to know where in the total mark range one is starting from in the effort to get that few extra marks, to know which is the high school one could be sure of getting into when one chooses to try for the school one notch higher.

School also teaches the pleasures of socialization, the shared pleasure of group accomplishment. It prepares people not only to accept as natural, but also to get comfort from, the patterns of co-operative effort, constant consultation, group responsibility and group sharing in achievement which seem to contribute to the efficiency of Japanese enterprises and to sustain their character as 'learning organisms'.

Many people have long since wondered whether the price which is paid for these advantages — the price exacted by the intense examination competition — is not too high. Parents, and even more, grandparents, of the middle class recall the days before such a high proportion of their fellow countrymen were taking part in the educational race — and before the latter-day commercial organization of the competition in mock tests and 'standard-deviation scores' brought the pressures of the entrance examination system down into primary school and kindergarten. They recall that they had time in their mid-teens for hobbies, for collecting insects, for mountain-climbing expeditions, for reading Dostoevsky. Contemporary children cannot afford to let up until they are safely settled in the best university they can get into. And by then they will have acquired sufficient distaste for anything that smacks of disinterested, non-career-related study that all they want is to earn enough from part-time jobs to buy a sports car or go on overseas trips. A comparative survey found considerably fewer high school students who said they ever read for pleasure even than in America (Grayson 1984a, 212).

These humanistic concerns alone have not hitherto been enough to move governments. But more recently, a new concern with scientific creativity has. The cost of all this effortful endeavour on the part of Japanese adolescents is now seen to be not just unhappiness, but low levels of individuality, creativity, capacity to take initiatives. And in a Japan which has now caught up with the advanced industrial powers and now has to do its own inventing, a Japan which has shown its material prowess and now feels the urge to prove itself in other ways — by winning Nobel prizes, for instance — this is seen to be serious. A new ad hoc committee reporting directly to the Prime Minister was set up in 1984 to make recommendations for the reform of the educational system.

The Commission deliberated for more than three years amid continuous publicity. It produced two interim reports and a final one. Its mild suggestions for reform, however, amount to nothing that could fundamentally alter the structure or dynamics of Japanese schools. It is not only that inertia of a high order is built into any educational system. No-one challenges the basic principles of meritocracy and equality of opportunity. (And why should they as, slowly, those principles penetrate more deeply into the institutions of other industrial societies?) Some would wish marginally to amend the scholastic definition of 'merit' which guides the society's selection mechanisms (for both further education and jobs.) But no-one would wish fundamentally to challenge it. The system has its own logic and inevitability, and it will not be easily altered.

2

Who goes where?

The next chapter will describe the wide range of vocational courses in Japanese high schools, colleges and universities — all within the mainline formal educational system under the Ministry of Education. Here, first, we consider who gets into them, why they get into them, and what getting into them does for self-image, learning motivations and employability.

What is taught in school and how good the teachers are at putting it across are important. But who learns it and why, whether by choice or because they have been 'relegated' to it, what that does on the one hand to their self-image and learning motivation; on the other hand to their labour-market image and employment chances — all these things are just as important for determining the cost-effectiveness of public expenditure on vocational education.

There are two problems about getting able children — the children who in almost any school system are offered the widest choice of educational opportunities — into vocational schools. One is the 'gentlemen do not involve themselves in trade' syndrome. (Or in the Confucian Analects version: 'Gentlemen steer clear of the kitchen'.) Healthy schools can only thrive in a society which believes that learning for its own sake is a good and morally applaudable activity. But in any society with a few centuries of literacy and a history of established class divisions behind it, that belief tends to become confused with the very different notion that learning for any other, instrumental, purpose is, if not exactly base and prostitutive, at least inferior — a notion which derives from aristocratic traditions of status assertion through conspicuous leisure and abstention from any pretensions to 'mere usefulness'. Hence, science is gentlemanly and engineering is for inferior breeds. And from Oxford, which derives in most direct continuity from an aristocratic past, even a professor of engineering can write to *The Times* to protest that his courses are *not* vocational (12 September 1972).

Let us call that the 'academic bias problem'. It is a problem at all branching points in a school system where there are choices — at university entry as well as at secondary school entry. But there is another problem, a special problem at the secondary level, which one might call the 'ability-labelling problem'. Where university entrance is competitive — and in any society it is competitive for the top institutions — selection is almost always by achievement in general education subjects. Those who spend a good part of their secondary schooling on vocational rather than on these core academic subjects are therefore prejudicing, if not abandoning, their chance of getting into a university — or at least a 'good' university.

In societies (let us call them A-type societies) where university education is still predominantly a small-enrolment preserve of the middle classes, and where, in the social circles in which a large proportion of the population moves, getting to a university is considered as a rather special and unusual achievement, there may be quite a lot of people who are very happy to abandon the chance of university entrance in favour of the chance to acquire a skill which offers what counts in their circles as a decent job.

Not so, in societies (B-type) where universities absorb a much higher proportion of the age group — the 40 per cent of the US or Japan, for example — where the aspiration to go to a university is widespread and the financial means of doing so widely available. There, teenagers may be much more reluctant to give up hopes of a university education by getting on the 'wrong' track; vocational schools are much more likely, therefore, to be second-best choices and to be populated by pupils who have been sent there because they did not get good enough marks to get into the school of their first choice.

There is a further complication. Employers may well be interested in recruiting people with specific kinds of knowledge, specific kinds of mental or manual skills. But they are also interested in other things — like general intelligence or capacity for effort. (And they are especially so interested in Japan because so much first-job recruitment is career recruitment for lifetime employment.) Academic achievement is often taken as a proxy measure of these qualities. And if — as in Japan — access to school places is strictly rationed by academic achievement through competitive entrance examinations, the school one has been to may be taken as a proxy measure of those important mental qualities. And where that is so, children and their parents may be even more hesitant to opt for a type of school which might brand them as low achievers, for fear of actually worsening their job chances in the labour market. (With the result that those schools become more completely second-choice schools than before, more likely to brand their pupils as low achievers, more desperately avoided by those who could do 'better' — and so on, down and down the vicious spiral.)

The two effects — the academic bias problem and the ability-labelling problem — are quite separate, and it confuses discussion not to treat them separately.

Japan is clearly on average a B-type society, with the exacerbating features of (a) meritocratic selection and (b) lifetime employment, which were mentioned in the last paragraph but one. It is not surprising that all the local parental pressure should have been directed at expanding general course, rather than vocational course provision; once 60 per cent of total places in 1955, the general courses had 72 per cent in 1985.

Vocational high schools, however, (or at least their technical courses, less so their commercial and even less so their agricultural courses) are saved from futility by four things. First, they are serious, well-run organizations whose older staff members were recruited at a time when Japan was still an A-type society and vocational schools had high prestige. Second, Japanese employers are not only interested in general intellectual ability besides substantive knowledge and skills; they are also interested in attitudes, and many will take entering, or at least buckling down to, a vocational high school course as an indication of highly desirable attitudes. Third, efforts have been made to keep open the road to the university, even for vocational course students. There remains a high general-education content in the vocational school courses, and the practice has grown (to be sure only in the lower reaches of the university prestige hierarchy) of admitting students from vocational schools by recommendation from their teachers — without requiring an entrance examination. Fourth, although Japan is on average a B-type society, it is not homogeneously so. There is a difference between a metropolitan prefecture like Tokyo where once some 60 per cent, now around 50 per cent, of an age group go to a university and the northern more rural prefectures where the proportion is between 20 and 30. The ability range on which the vocational high schools draw is a good deal higher in the latter areas, the more so since the vocational schools are nearly all public, and greater prestige attaches to getting into a public high school, more especially in poorer areas where there are fewer high-prestige private

15

Table 2.1 Employers' attitudes to graduates of high schools: technical, commercial, ordinary

A. *Manufacturing sector* (N = 261)

Q. Have you recruited THS technical high school graduates in the last 2 to 3 years?

Yes	40.8%
No	59.2%

Q. If yes, what was the main reason for recruiting?

1. Expected specialist knowledge and skill	78.9%
2. Expected that THS graduates would have excellent attitudes, in terms of willingness to work and inter-personal relations	7.4%
3. The fact that recruits were THS graduates was not a positive reason for hiring	10.5%
4. Other and no reply	3.2%

Q. In the event that your establishment recruits ordinary high school graduates in future, which, between THS graduates and OHS graduates, would you prefer?

THS graduates	66.4%
OHS graduates	9.4%
Either	19.7%
Other	4.5%

Q. If THS graduates, what is the main reason?

1. They possess specialist knowledge and skill	62.8%
2. They have better attitudes to work	2.7%
3. Some jobs are too difficult for OHS graduates	31.1%
4. Other	3.4%

Q. If OHS graduates, what is the main reason?

3. They possess excellent general, basic knowledge	13.6%
2. They may be trained in-house to do various types of jobs	86.4%
3. They have future potential	0%
4. Other	0%

B. Services Sector (N = 331)

Q. Have you recruited CHS (commercial high school) graduates in the last 2 to 3 years?

Yes	Male 36.9%	Female 53.0%	
No	Male 63.1%	Female 47.0%	

Q. If yes, what was the main reason for recruiting?

	Male	Female
1. Expected specialist knowledge and skill in administration, sales and data-processing	28.5	34.2
2. Expected that CHS graduates would have excellent attitudes, in terms of willingness to work and inter-personal relations	18.6	17.5
3. The fact that recruits were CHS graduates was not a positive reason for hiring	48.0	38.9
4. Other	4.9	9.4

Q. In the event that your establishment recruits high school graduates in future which, as between CHS graduates and ordinary high school graduates, would you prefer?

	Male	Female
CHS graduates	25.6	35.6
OHS graduates	16.0	10.0
Either	52.1	50.2
Other	6.3	4.2

Q. If CHS graduates, why?

	Male	Female
1. Possess specialist knowledge & skill	59.7	68.8
2. Better attitudes to work	24.2	19.4
3. Some jobs are difficult for OHS graduates	11.3	9.7
4. Other	4.8	2.1

Q. If OHS graduates, why?

	Male	Female
1. Possess good general, basic knowledge	26.3	38.3
2. Can train in-house to do certain jobs	65.8	46.2
3. They have future potentials	2.6	7.7
4. Other	5.3	7.6

Source: Ministry of Education, Committee on Science Education and Industrial Education, *The future of vocational education in high schools* 1985 (Survey of August 1983)

schools and the cost advantages of public education intensify the entry competition. This serves to moderate any tendency to put the 'place for the dumb kids' label on vocational schools in general, but it also means that the employment prospects and destinations of vocational school graduates vary in different parts of the country. Table 2.1, which reports survey figures regarding employers' assessments of the products of vocational schools, only tells an average story; the detailed picture is more complicated.

These points can only be made clear by an explanation of the mechanics of the selection process.

THE SLICING SYSTEM

The Japanese revert to sausages rather than to bottles of non-homogenized milk when they want a metaphor for ability selection, and for a very good reason. The 'slicing' of the age group into ability-homogeneous segments goes all the way down the spectrum; it is not just a matter of creaming off the top quarter.

As described in the last chapter, mixed-ability teaching is the over-whelmingly dominant practice until compulsory education ends at age 15. The slicing process takes place, first, when pupils are allocated at that age to high-prestige, indifferent, or low-prestige high schools, and secondly, for 37 per cent of them (41 per cent of boys and 35 per cent of girls), when they are allocated at the age of 18–19 between high-, medium- or low-prestige universities or in the case of girls, between co-educational universities for about two-thirds of them, or sheltered single-sex universities for the rest.

Let us take the first great sort-out which leads some to general academic and some to vocational high schools — or, rather, to courses in those high schools, since some are comprehensive. In most prefectures the system is as follows.

All public high schools recruit selectively from those pupils with the highest marks in the common prefecture-wide entrance examination (an examination in all five main school subjects — Japanese, maths, English, general science and social studies) who have put their school as their first choice. They consider second-choice applicants only if first-choice applicants do not fill all their places, and since there are not enough public high school places for all the pupils in the relevant age group (and a good number end up in inferior spill-over private schools) this does not often happen. Prudence, therefore, counsels making one's first choice a school in which one is likely to be successful.

Table 2.2(a) Destinations of upper secondary school graduates, 1984

	Further education	Employment	Special training schools & miscellaneous schools	Other	Total (thousands)
	%	%	%	%	
All courses	29.6	39.8	25.1	5.4	1,482
A. General	38.2	25.2	30.6	6.1	399
B. Vocational total	7.9	76.5	11.8	3.7	425
Agriculture	6.5	77.4	13.4	2.7	48
Industry	7.5	80.2	10.0	2.3	140
Commerce	6.6	78.9	10.1	4.4	178
Fisheries	8.8	80.6	8.2	2.4	5
Home economics	13.4	62.5	17.1	7.0	46
Nursing	21.4	33.0	43.5	2.2	8
C. Other	56.4	11.9	25.3	6.5	11

Source: *Basic School Survey*
N.B. Percentages may not add up to 100.0 due to rounding.

Table 2.2(b) Destinations of full-time technical high school graduates

Industry course graduates only	1973	1977	1981	1985
	%	%	%	%
a. Employment	77.7	73.6	80.4	81.5
b. Employment and part-time study	1.6	1.4	0.9	0.7
c. University and junior colleges	10.5	12.5	8.5	6.8
d. Special training schools	4.2	7.1	7.1	8.2
e. Vocational training schools	0	0	0.6	0.6
f. Other (e.g. studying to retake entrance exams)	6	5.4	2.5	2.2
g. Total graduates	100	100	100	100

Source: Survey by the Association of Technical High School Headmasters

19

Most pupils are able to do this, thanks to the elaborate diagnostic system which has been developed over the years. In the last two years of middle school, pupils take a dozen or more mock tests. (These are provided by commercial firms in the prefecture, mostly staffed by ex-teachers.) All test marks are standardized on the whole 14-year-old population of the prefecture in a generally understood fashion — 10 marks above or below 50 for each standard deviation — so that only five per cent come above 70 or below 30. Since children's effort input tends to be fairly uniform there is a relative stability in each child's scores — his or her *hensachi* range, or range of 'standard-deviation scores' tends to be rather narrow.

It is on the basis of these scores that teachers initially advise their children whether they should apply for a 'top' or a 'middling' or a 'lower-range' high school. What happens then varies. For one thing there is considerable variation between prefectures in the size of the catchment areas within which the sorting is done. In some prefectures with large school districts — a single catchment pool for eight or more schools, say — all the middle school teachers in charge of final year classes spend a horse-trading weekend where, in the light of the range of scores of their charges they hammer out quotas, first of all for the top school, in such a way as to equalize the scores of the marginal lowest-scoring pupil from each school. Then they do the same for the second-best school, and so on down the line. Over the next weeks they advise their pupils and their pupils' parents accordingly. An alternative is to allow initial tentative applications, then for each high school to publish statistics of applicant numbers, thus allowing the weaker candidates to be withdrawn from over-subscribed schools, before definitive applications are sent in.

How this works in practice in a rural area with a relatively low rate of progression to university may be illustrated by the situation in Iwaki city in Fukushima prefecture, which is the subject of Table 2.3. It is a bigger-than-average catchment area, where the ranking of high schools is unambiguous. At what one might call Level 1, there is a single top public school for boys and one for girls which between them take about 17 per cent of the age group. (Some of the northern prefectures — unlike any in central and western Japan — still partially hold out against co-education.) These two schools owe their pre-eminence to the fact that they were the only pre-war selective secondary schools in the district. Almost all of the boys and the majority of the girls who attend them go on subsequently to college or university.

At Level 2, there is a third general academic-course high school

Figure 2.1 Progression routes in the Japanese Educational System, 1985

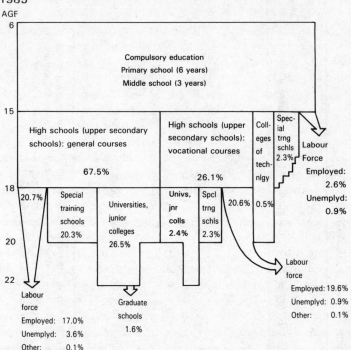

Source: Ministry of Education. *Mombu tokei yoran*, (summary of statistics on education) 1985
N.B. Special Training Schools include, as well as Special Training Schools (senshu-gakko) proper, also Miscellaneous Schools (kakushu-gakko) and Ministry of Labour Vocational Training Schools (shokugyo kunrenko).

which takes both boys and girls and from which about a third of the leavers seek to, and manage to, get into (lesser) universities. Also on Level 2 are two of the vocational schools — an industrial technical school which takes predominantly boys, and a commercial vocational school which takes predominantly girls. They rank as of approximately equal prestige with the general-course high school just mentioned, and are in fact slightly more difficult to get into — in the case of the Data Processing Course at the technical school, much more difficult. A third technical school in another part of the district has a slightly lower entrance level.

Then, at Level 3 come three general high schools which divide up the next slice of the age group (roughly from the 50th to the 80th

Table 2.3 Hensachi distribution of public senior high schools in Iwaki City, 1986

Marginal Hensachi*	General		All Vocational		Technical**		Commercial**		Other Vocational***		College of Technology	
66-												
61-65												
56-60	468	(17.4)	70	(4.0)							70	(51.9)
51-5	464	(17.2)	65	(3.7)							65	(48.1)
46-55	451	(16.7)	549	(31.2)	235	(32.9)	314	(55.3)				
41-45			526	(29.9)	440	(61.6)	86	(15.1)				
36-40			39	(2.2)	39	(5.5)						
31-35	640	(23.7)	237	(13.5)			168	(29.6)	69	(20.2)		
30 or less	672	(24.9)	272	(15.5)					272	(79.8)		
Total	2,695	(100.0)	1,758	(100.0)	714	(100.0)	568	(100.0)	341	(100.0)	135	(100.0)

Grand total: 4,453

*The hensachi score of the lowest-scoring pupil admitted to the school. Hensachi = the standardized average score over third-year mock tests (standardized by the formula: 50 plus or minus the number of standard deviations from the mean multiplied by 10).
**For all vocational schools, the marginal hensachi is that for each course, rather than for the school as a whole.
***Other vocational school courses are agricultural, fishery and domestic service courses.

Table 2.4 Hensachi distribution of public senior high schools in Tokyo Prefecture, 1983

Marginal Hensachi*	Numbers of schools					
	General		Technical**		Commercial**	
66-	2	(1.4)				
61-65	20	(13.9)				
56-60	26	(18.1)				
51-55	34	(23.6)	4	(4.8)	2	(9.1)
46-50	30	(20.8)	12	(14.5)	2	(9.1)
41-45	30	(20.8)	33	(39.8)	16	(72.7)
36-40	2	(1.4)	28	(33.7)	2	(9.1)
35 or less			6	(7.2)		
Total	144	(100.0)	83	(100.0)	22	(100.0)

*The hensachi score of the lowest-scoring pupil admitted to the school. Hensachi = the standardized average score over third-year mock tests (standardized by the formula: 50 plus or minus the number of standard deviations from the mean multiplied by 10).
**For all vocational schools, the marginal hensachi is that for each course, rather than for the school as a whole.
***Other vocational school courses are agricultural, fishery and domestic service courses.

percentile of the ability range) primarily on geographical lines, and below them — Level 4 — two general schools which try to fill their places by a 'second round recruitment' — scooping up those who failed to get into their first-choice school higher up the pecking order. Finally, at the bottom of the public school heap are two vocational schools — one for agriculture and one for fisheries.

There are no elite university-preparatory private schools within commuting distance of this area — a major difference from the situation in areas where (at a rough guess) some 80 per cent of the population lives. There are just two private high schools. They take children who cannot get into any public high school even at the second-round recruitment, or children who could get into a low-ranking public school, but whose parents would prefer them to be educated with the children of other parents who can afford private school fees. This syndrome is stronger in the case of girls — what they learn is less important for their life chances/marriage chances than who they learn it with. The girls' private school, in consequence, may have pupils who could have got into Level 3 schools.

The only further complication: there is one school with all-prefecture recruitment — the five-year College of Technology — in the prefectural capital at some considerable distance and hence for boarders only as far as Iwaki is concerned. The small number of Iwaki pupils who go there would have had a good chance (in the case of those entering the machinery and construction courses) or an almost certain chance (in the case of those entering the more popular electricity or applied chemistry courses) of getting into the Level 1 high schools. But they are unlikely to be in that top five per cent of scorers whose teachers would tell them they had a good chance of going on from high school to a good national university.

It is obvious that it makes little sense to compare the average abilities of general-course students and vocational-course students: some general courses take the brightest, some the least bright children. One might summarize Iwaki's ability-distribution system as follows:

For a child diagnosed as being in the top 10 per cent of the ability distribution, it will be difficult to resist the pressure of teachers' urgings that 'of course' they should go to one of the top high schools and on to university — unless something in their connections or background makes the College of Technology alternative more attractive. (The 'ability labelling effect' makes the top schools attractive even for those who might not be able to afford to go to a university.)

For pupils who fall in the 10th to the 20th percentile, there is a choice between:

— Aiming at the top school, and being prepared to take a year in a cramming school in order to get in at a second attempt.
— For those who cannot afford that, aiming at the top school and risking relegation to Level 3 or 4 if the bid fails.
— Aiming at one of the Level 2 schools — the general school or one of the 3 vocational schools — with near certainty of success.

For those who fall in the 20th to the 50th percentile range (a rather narrow range in performance terms) application to a top school is a big risk. They are naturals for the Level 2 schools and provide the bulk of the entrants to the vocational schools.

As to what determines choice as between general and vocational courses in this ability range, there are few careful studies, it being, apparently, very difficult for Japanese educational sociologists to do any work correlating performance with social class characteristics except at the broadest ecological level. (See e.g. Hata 1975–6.) Clearly important are: sex (it is more important for boys to go to university, but, on the other hand, general courses have higher general prestige and so are better for ladylike marriageability); the family's economic circumstances (keeping a child in a Tokyo university can cost well over half of the average Iwaki family's income); the general level of social aspiration — white collar families are more likely to make sacrifices to push a moderately bright child into the university-going bracket, blue collar families to think that their child might as well learn something useful; and parental occupation — families with small businesses want their eldest sons to learn something of use to the business, private doctors' and dentists' sons aspire to enter father's profession.

In a metropolitan prefecture like Tokyo where social aspiration levels are higher and universities more cheaply accessible to those who can commute from home, a much higher proportion of the high school population is bent on taking a general course and keeping open their options for university entry. Hence the vocational school students come from lower down the ability range, as Table 2.4 shows. The 'image' of the vocational high schools is less favourable, and employers' eagerness to recruit from them is diminished — quite apart from any doubts they might harbour about the usefulness of what is taught in such schools or the quality of their teaching — doubts which might apply equally in Iwaki as in Tokyo.

UNIVERSITY ENTRY

Vocational courses at the university do not suffer so obviously from any 'ability-labelling' problem, and the extent to which the 'academic bias problem' is evident is limited. Japan has no Oxfords and no Cambridges. Its elite universities have never been places where reverend clerks prepared young gentlemen for a life of, hopefully cultured, indolence, or nobility-obliged public service. They started off — just at the time when the feudal aristocracy was being pensioned off and winkled out of its land rights — as meritocratic as the *grandes écoles*, and they were built for a country which took industrialization, and especially manufacturing, seriously. The cultural break with the past which the political upheaval of the 1860s and 1870s brought, immeasurably weakened Confucian notions about gentlemen and kitchens. Engineering as well as science was an integral part of the first university foundations.

As between arts stream and science stream, therefore, there is little difference either in prestige, or in material prospects. A science graduate from a university which just misses being a top-rate university is more likely to end up on the board of a major manufacturing

25

Table 2.5 University places available by subject and rating of university, 1986

University places available, 1986, by subject and rating of university for science and engineering.

Rank: 'standard deviation score' rating	Physical Sciences		Mechanical Engineering		Electrical & Electronic Engineering		Civil Engineering		Chemical Engineering		Other Engineering	
	Public	Private	Public	Private	Public	Private	Public	Private	Public	Private	Public	Private
A (68.0+)	762 (5.6)	1,171 (8.6)	678 (6.0)	672 (5.9)	551 (4.0)	810 (5.9)	293 (2.4)	0	331 (8.0)	0	1,794 (14.4)	21 (0.2)
B (60–67.9)	4,183 (30.7)	1,540 (11.3)	2,480 (21.8)	660 (5.8)	3,389 (24.8)	1,150 (8.4)	1,761 (14.5)	466 (3.8)	1,470 (35.3)	350 (8.4)	3,820 (30.7)	97 (0.8)
C (55–59.9)	1,636 (12.0)	1,222 (9.0)	1,106 (9.7)	1,092 (9.6)	547 (4.0)	1,649 (12.1)	1,156 (9.5)	910 (7.5)	456 (10.0)	370 (8.9)	2,026 (16.3)	78 (0.6)
D (50–54.9)	560 (4.2)	1,650 (12.1)	0	1,910 (16.7)	0	1,960 (14.4)	0	1,740 (14.3)	0	465 (11.1)	780 (6.3)	1,297 (10.4)
E (up to 49.9)	0	870 (6.4)	0	2,790 (24.5)	0	3,590 (26.3)	0	5,860 (48.1)	0	720 (17.3)	0	2,545 (20.4)
Total	13,594 (100)		11,388 (100)		13,646 (100)		12,186 (100)		4,162 (100)		12,458 (100)	

Comparison of university places, 1986, for two types of course

Rank: 'standard deviation score' rating	Science and engineering			Economics and business studies		
	Public	Private	Total	Public	Private	Total
A (68.0+)	4,409 (14.8)	2,674 (7.1)	7,083 (10.5)	1,230 (6.3)	3,140 (6.9)	4,370 (6.7)
B (60.0-67.9)	17,103 (57.4)	4,263 (11.3)	21,366 (31.7)	6,854 (34.9)	7,560 (16.5)	14,414 (22.1)
C (55-59.9)	6,972 (23.3)	5,321 (14.1)	12,293 (18.2)	1,125 (5.7)	10,940 (23.9)	12,065 (18.5)
D (50-54.9)	1,340 (4.5)	9,022 (24.0)	10,362 (15.4)	10,415 (53.1)	870 (1.9)	11,285 (17.3)
E (up to 49.9)	0	16,375 (43.5)	16,375 (24.3)	0	23,205 (50.8)	23,205 (35.5)
Total	29,824 (100.0)	37,655 (100.0)	67,479 (100)	19,624 (100)	45,715 (100)	65,339 (100)

Source: Ron Dore, 'Where will the Japanese Nobel prizes come from?' *Science and Public Policy* vol. 13, no. 6, December 1986
N.B. Percentages may not add to 100.0 due to rounding.

company — and probably just as likely to get a job as a MITI civil servant — as somebody from the very top of the arts/social science tree — a graduate of the law department of Tokyo University, say. In fact, those who show themselves good enough at maths will, in many school environments, have to be quite single-minded to resist the assumption of teachers and parents that of course they should try to get a science place.

Anyone trying for a place at a national university does not have to make a definite choice of stream until he writes out his entrance application forms: the first-hurdle national examination is in the five main subjects — maths, science and social studies for everybody. For the private universities, however, entrance examinations are in three subjects only (excluding either science and maths, or social studies and Japanese), so there is generally some specialization — in the private high schools — from the age of 16 or 17. The non-chosen subjects are not entirely dropped, however, so that a change of stream is not too difficult at 18.

The hensachi system permits some objective measure of the attractiveness of different subjects and their consequent ability to recruit able students. The advertising literature of the cram schools (which are attended by *ronin* students making a second or third attempt at entrance exams as well as by current high school students) rate each university department by the hensachi score which should guarantee an 80 per cent chance of success in its entrance examination. (The figures are produced by analysing the 'average mock test scores' of the previous year's applicants and the difference in scores between those who passed and those who failed each department's entrance examination.) From these figures it seems, if one takes the top university, Tokyo, that entrance scores for the Law/Political Science Faculty and for the Science and Engineering Faculty are about equal, and both several points below the Medical Faculty. (The intense competition to enter all medical schools — in some of the less savoury reaches of the private university system, competition in parental donations to the Building Fund as well as in marks — is a reflection of the high incomes which doctors enjoy in Japan.)

Table 2.5 uses these ratings — as given by the brochure of one cram school chain — to compare the national distribution by ability rankings of pupils in economics on the one hand, and of various branches of science and engineering on the other. It makes the point that the latter are on average brighter, but in both subjects the dispersal is wide. There are a good number of students graduating from private provincial engineering colleges whose academic achievement levels are not much above average for the whole ability range, and well below average for the university-going group. They are likely to be recruited by local small building firms and manufacturing companies for careers which would look more like technicians' careers in Britain. Likewise, or even more so, the lesser-university economists.

Within science and engineering there is certainly evidence of the 'academic bias'. But again it gets intermixed with the 'ability level effect'. Where physics is established as the prestige subject par excellence — as it was made in Japan by the nation's first two Nobel prizes — then that is where the cream of the cream go. And getting into physics then becomes the only way of publicly demonstrating that you are the cream of the cream.

Again there are objective indicators of differential values, albeit at the local level. Tokyo University recruits all its science and engineering students through two entrance examinations, one for the physical and one for the biological sciences. Specialization starts at the beginning of the third year, and students are allocated to their first-choice department according to their marks in the first two years' courses. Physics is, indeed, the elite department which it is most difficult to get into, and it is some of the less prestigious engineering departments like civil engineering which scoop up the left-overs. But equally, some of the engineering departments — aeronautical engineering, for example — are near the top of the tree.

And that is, after all, an elite university pattern — the pattern at a university whose graduates can expect, if they survive among the quarter of the intake who are admitted to the PhD course, to have no difficulty in pursuing an academic career — albeit as teachers at a provincial university. At universities further down the ability/prestige ladder — even among the less than a dozen universities to which PhD courses are confined — this attraction of the academic, pure-science stream is less evident. As will be seen from the overall distribution pattern shown in Table 2.5, although science and maths students do have better academic records than engineering students, the difference is not very great.

It is also relevant that the science graduates of lesser universities and those who do not make it into the graduate courses of the elite universities, have little hesitation in going into industry after they graduate. The tendency noted in other countries for finance houses, merchant banks and stock-broking companies to snap up the best and the brightest of them was almost unknown in Japan until 1987 when the internationalization of finance and the euphoria of five years of bull markets finally produced yuppie-level salary offers from the securities companies, and the newspaper leader writers began to deplore the corruption of hitherto healthy Japanese capitalism. Are those they asked, who make money finally going to have higher prestige than those who make products? Is Japan finally treading the primrose path that led to Britain's decline?

LIFETIME EARNINGS

It may seem strange, to those used to orthodox analysis by economists of the rates of return on investment in a university degree, that Japanese youth should be so preoccupied with climbing the educational ladder when, as Figure 2.2 shows, the lifetime earnings of university graduates are not so superior to those of high school graduates. The differential is smaller, in fact, than in almost any other country.

Figure 2.2 Educational level and earnings of university graduates, 1976–85

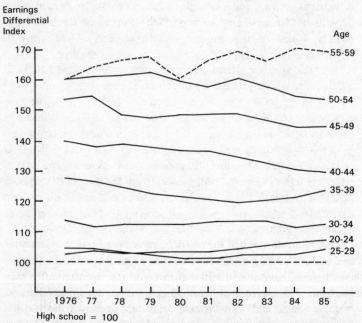

Source: Rodosho, seisaku-chosa-bu (Ministry of Labour, Policy Research Bureau). *Chingin, rōdō-jikan seido tō sogō-chōsa hōkoku* (Survey of wages, hours and conditions of service), 1984

Table 2.6 Lifetime earnings by educational level and size of firm, 1985

University Graduates [Overall = 100]				
Enterprises employing	*Base Pay*	*Bonuses*	*Pensions*	*Total*
> 1,000	100	100	100	100
300-999	88	80	80	85
100-299	84	74	68	80
< 100	82	67	66	77
High School Graduates: Clerical, Admin. [Overall = 95]				
> 1,000	100	100	100	100
300-999	94	86	96	91
100-299	89	78	79	85
< 100	89	67	70	81
High School Graduates: Production Workers [Overall = 82]				
> 1,000	100	100	100	100
300-999	101	98	108	101
100-299	91	81	80	87
< 100	89	67	70	81

Source: Calculations by Recruit Research Ltd. These are undiscounted summations of cross-sectional data for 1985.

Table 2.7 Wage differentials by size of establishment

Establishments employing:	1970	1980	1985
More than 500 workers	100.0	100.0	100.0
100-499 workers	81.5	80.5	77.1
30-99 workers	81.6	65.3	62.9
5-29 workers	61.8	58.0	54.9

Source: Keizai Kikakucho (Economic Planning Agency), *Keizai yoran (Summary of economic statistics)*, 1986, p. 154.

The answer, of course, is that the usual statistics — showing, for instance, that the average high school graduate may be getting 95 per cent of the lifetime earnings of a university graduate — tell only half the story. What counts is which high school and which university. Only top universities open the door to top firms, and so on. Some inkling of the difference it makes may be seen in the differentials by size of enterprise shown in Tables 2.6 and 2.7, if one assumes that size of enterprise (number of employees) can stand as a rough proxy measure of prestige, monopoly power, and profitability.

31

There may be indications, too, that the overall university-graduation premium may be on the increase again. At least that is a possible interpretation of the lines in Figure 2.2 which shows that the high school/university earnings differential has been somewhat increasing in recent years in the younger age groups.

One can certainly think of a plausible reason for this to happen. One might assume that the factors affecting university entry have changed. Once it was very much a matter of family finances rather than scholastic ability when those now in their fifties were coming out of school. In today's more affluent society it has become much more a matter of ability and less of capacity to pay. Hence older generations of high school graduates could have contained large numbers of very able people (whose ability-level counterparts would nowadays be fairly certain to go to a good university) whose abilities have won them considerable promotion within their companies.

Only time will tell what foundation this speculation has. If one can swallow the assumption that pay reflects marginal productivity, it is at least consistent with the observation of a senior engineer on the success of the quality circles (work process improvement circles) in his factory. He attributed a lot to the initiative, the leadership, the sustained level of intellectual curiosity, and the inventiveness of some of his senior foremen. 'And they left school at fifteen — at twelve some of the older ones. One never seems to get people of that calibre coming out of high school into our blue collar jobs these days.'

That can serve as a final reminder of the pervasive implications of the mechanisms to the description of which this chapter has been devoted. The way education and training systems sort and label people and thereby influence their occupational destinations is a very important aspect of those systems. It rivals and (for a society's economic functioning at least) may even surpass in importance the aspect to which attention is more frequently devoted — the way schools seek to influence the intellectual (as well as the aesthetic and moral) development of their charges.

3

Vocational streams in the mainline formal education system

THE SECONDARY LEVEL

High schools which offer nothing but vocational courses made up 16 per cent of the 5,453 total in 1985. They are called industrial, commercial, agricultural, music, etc. high schools, according to their specialty. There were another 31 per cent of schools with some (minority) vocational streams, leaving just over a half of schools which have only general academic courses.

Rarely do vocational schools offer a single type of course; some provide up to ten different ones. The Ministry of Education classified the 3,694 courses available in 1985 in the following 'course groups', as it calls them:

	%
Business-related	32.3
Industry-related	22.7
Home economics	19.0
Agriculture-related	13.0
Nursing	4.4
Fisheries	1.5
Other	7.1

The 1.44m pupils on vocational courses in 1985 made up 28 per cent of the total in high schools. (They had numbered 0.93m in 1955 and 2.05m in 1965 — then, in both years, 40% of the total.) Sex-typing is marked. Boys predominate in the industrial, girls in the business courses. Nearly four per cent of vocational school pupils are on four-year part-time evening courses. They were established

for youngsters who could not afford to be out of the labour market, and full-time-working youth once made up a large part of their clientele. Some were established by, or in co-operation with, groups of local manufacturers for the 15-year-olds they recruited from rural areas and housed in their factory dormitories; some indeed still survive in that form. But increasingly they are the last resort of the children who cannot get a full-time place in a public high school in areas where they are scarce, and who cannot afford to go to a private spill-over school, nor, often, manage to get a full-time job either. Some manage an early transfer to a full-time school place; others get a job (these schools are obvious places for employers to come recruiting) and may or may not keep up with their studies. Proportions graduating — from the part-time as well as from among the 133,000 registered for correspondence courses — are not high. Rohlen's *Japan's High Schools* describes graphically the somewhat dispiriting atmosphere of one such school.

SPECIALIZATIONS

Vocational high school courses are quite specialized. Among the industry-related courses, the most common specializations are machinery, electricity, electronics, architecture, and civil engineering, but other more specialized courses include: automobile repair, metalwork, textiles, interior furnishings, design, printing, precision machinery, radio communication, and welding. New courses in (primarily the hardware of) information technology are expanding, and the Advisory Council which oversees these schools recommended a new course in mechatronics (the Japanese word for devices, using sensors and transducers, which involve both electronic and mechanical processes). In terms of hensachi entrance points, the most difficult courses to get into are information technology, electronics, electricity and machinery, in that order.

There is a smaller range of choice among the business-related courses, the most numerous being general commerce, data processing (the most popular and difficult to get into), accountancy and administration. The history of the commerce course offers an interesting illustration of the interaction between economic change and educational change. It was once reckoned an excellent training for the sons, daughters and prospective wives of small businessmen. And there were enough of them around for demand to be quite high and entry difficult. This meant that the academically able graduates of such courses were in demand, also, from good companies which were keen to hire them as clerks. The attractions of the small-business life declined, however (both for income and security reasons, and because in a more affluent society family duty weighed less heavily and girls could more easily claim the chance to savour the somewhat romanticized pleasures of office life). At the same time the expansion of universities increased the relative attractions of the general courses. Companies came to prefer to get their white-collar workers from the general courses rather than from the commercial courses. The attractions — and hensachi entrance levels — of the commerce courses further declined, and their providers have tried the desperate remedy of trying to make them as much like general courses as possible, thereby holding out the promise of going on to junior college.

As the wits have it: in the Tokugawa period, the four orders of society were *shi-no-ko-sho* — samurai, farmer (agriculturalist), artisan (industrialist) and merchant (commercant) — in that order of social worth; today in the high schools the rank order is *fu-sho-ko-no* — general, commercial, industrial, agricultural, with the once highly regarded schools for farm children unequivocally at the bottom of the heap. Keeping the youngsters down on the farm has long since been given up as a feasible proposition by all but a handful of Japanese farm families. Until the late 1950s the assumption was that all eldest sons stayed on the farm. Later, as younger labour shortage developed in the 1960s, industry and services began, not only to gobble up the younger sons, but to offer attractive places for the eldest sons as well. By the end of that decade, it was a rare 15-year-old who went willingly to an agricultural high school. As in the Iwaki example described in the last chapter, in most such schools — and they remain numerous — there is still strong ideological resistance to any attempt to demote agriculture in the social scheme of things, and they have become scoop-up schools at the bottom of the prestige ladder. This applies not only to the common courses like general agriculture, farm home economics, horticulture, civil engineering, forestry, etc., but also to more specialized courses in tea growing, apple growing and silkworm farming. One exception, one bright spot in an otherwise gloomy picture, is the popularity of courses in food manufacturing and food chemistry, which have gained from the attention directed towards biotechnology.

The other course groups, briefly, are:

The fisheries course group, comprising general fisheries, fish product processing, radio communication, fishing boat operation.

The home economics course group comprises varied specialized courses in home management, garment-making, food and nutrition, child-rearing.

The nursing course group is in fact a single course — that leading to the auxiliary nursing certificate.

HOW VOCATIONAL?

The Ministry stipulation is that at least one-third of total school hours should be devoted to general education subjects (Japanese, social studies, maths, science, physical education, art and, compulsorily but only for girls, home economics). In actual practice these subjects — plus English — consume about a half of total school hours. Maths, for instance, usually gets four 50-minute periods a week in the first year and three in the second, and, though in industry-related subjects only, the same number in the third when pupils learn to integrate and differentiate.

Options are as rare in the vocational schools as in the general high schools; the choice within social studies among Japanese history, world history and geography is about all that is allowed. As suggested in Chapter 1, equality of opportunity for progression to higher education is one reason for this uniformity, but that hardly explains why the Ministry should be so concerned to extend it to the first two years of university, too. (To the point that Ministry officials would not countenance a TV University of the Air, unless it made provision for including physical education as a compulsory part of its curriculum!) Ideals of the well-rounded individual have a lot to do with this, and well-rounded Japanese individuals are expected to be familiar, not only with the basic common stock of knowledge of their own society and history, but also with the language of numbers. Another factor in the lack of optional subjects is the belief that expending effort on subjects one does not necessarily enjoy is a very good training for life — life being rather more about performing one's duties than about pursuing happiness. When the economy becomes people-centred, then will be the time for the curriculum to become child-centred.

Effort, self-restraint, will-power, pushing oneself to attain in every field what are counted as minimum acceptable standards, play an important part in the not-so-hidden curriculum at many of these schools. The first school year at Kuramae, Tokyo's show-place technical school, includes a compulsory two-week 'swimming retreat', which builds up to the last day's mass-formation two-kilometre swim. Children who have never swum before, or are somewhat lacking in stamina need have no fear. Teachers surrounding the formation in small boats will fish them out of the water if they get into difficulties, and not put them back until they have massaged them back to life. (But note how thus they ensure that everybody can join in the triumphal singing on the bus back home.)

As for the vocational half of the curriculum, the Ministry's guidelines — in the case of industrial, agricultural and fishery courses — require that more of the time should be spent doing practical work than in the classroom. They are equally insistent on, though less specific about, practical work in the other courses. Very rarely, in the case of industrial and business courses, does practical work involve any experience in actual factories or offices. Work experience was once very popular in the late 1950s and early 1960s when companies were keen to recruit as many vocational high school graduates in short supply as possible. This is not the case these days as stagnant economic growth coupled with the tainted image of technical high school graduates (as being secondary in quality to general school graduates) has led companies to regard work experience provision as more of a burden than a mechanism for securing competent labour. However, pupils on cooking courses help out in office, factory and hospital canteens, and those doing nursing or childcare go to hospitals and day-care centres for practice.

Tables 3.1(a) and 3.1(b) list specimen curricula for four courses. The machinery and electricity curricula are from the Kuramae Technical High School mentioned earlier, the commerce and accounting curricula from the Taira Commercial High School in Iwaki.

CLASSROOM VERSUS PRACTICAL WORK: TECHNICAL HIGH SCHOOLS

It is not easy to discover the number of hours spent on practical and experimental work simply from looking at curricula. Some subjects are taught partly through the teacher giving basic instructions in the classroom, while the rest of the time is spent practising on machines. Overall, however, the Ministry's guidelines which require at least half the time allocated to vocational subjects to be spent on practice appear to be generally observed.

Two vocational subjects are compulsory and common to all THS courses, namely the Fundamentals of Industry and Industrial Mathematics. The object of Fundamentals is said to be:

Table 3.1 (a) Curriculum at a technical high school
(Unit: credit = 35 [50-minute] hours)

Subject area	Subject	General Subjects			Total
		Year 1	Year 2	Year 3	
Japanese language	Japanese Language I	4			4
Social Studies	Contemporary society		2	3	5
	World history	2	2		4
	Geography			3	3
Mathematics	Mathematics I	4			4
	Basic analysis		3		3
	Differentiation and integration			2	2
Science	Science I	4			4
	Physics		2	2	4
	Chemistry		2		2
P.E.	Physical Education	2	2	3	7
	Health	1	1		2
Art	Music I/Art I	2			2
English	English I	3			3
	English II		3		3
General subjects Total		22	17	13	52

Vocational Subjects

Subject	Engineering Course				Electrical course			
	Year 1	Year 2	Year 3	Total	Year 1	Year 2	Year 3	Total
Fundamentals of industry	4			4	3			3
Practice		4	4	8		4	6	10
Drawing	3	3	4	10		2	2	4
Industrial mathematics	2			2	2			2
Machine engineering work		2	2	4				
Machine design	1	2	3	6				
Prime movers		2	2	4				
Basic electricity		2		2	5	3		8
Electrical technology I						3	4	7
Electrical technology II						3	3	6
Vocational subjects Totals				40				40

Up to 4 optional credits may be taken from either the general or the vocational menu

Table 3.1(b) Curriculum at a commercial high school
(Unit: credit = 35 [50-minute] hours)

Subject area and Subject	Commerce				Accountancy			
	Year 1	Year 2	Year 3	Total	Year 1	Year 2	year 3	Total
Japanese language								
Japanese language I	3	1		4	3	1		4
Japanese language II		4		4		2	3	5
Language expression			(2)	(2)				
Modern prose			3	3				
Classics			3	3				
Social studies								
Contemporary society	4			4	4			4
Japanese history			5	5			3	3
World history						3		3
Geography		3(2)		3(2)				
Mathematics								
Mathematics I	3	3		6	3	3	2	8
Mathematics II			2	2				
Science								
Science I	3	3		6	3	3		6
Physical Education								
P.E. I	2	2	3	7	2	2	3	7
Health	1	1		2	1	1		2
Art								
Art I/Music I	2			2	2			2

Subject area and Subject	Commerce				Accountancy			
	Year 1	Year 2	Year 3	Total	Year 1	Year 2	year 3	Total
English								
English I	4			4	4	4	5	13
English II		6	6	12				
Home Economics								
General H.E.		(2)	(2)	(4)		(2)	(2)	(4)
General subjects Total	22	25	24	71	22	19(2)	16(2)	57(4)
Business								
Business economy I	3			3	3			3
Bookkeeping and accounting I	4			4	4			4
Bookkeeping and accounting II		3		3		3	2	5
Computing work	3	2		5	3	2		5
Data processing I			2	2			3	3
Comprehensive practice		2	3	5		3	4	7
Business laws and regulations			3	3			3	3
Industrial bookkeeping						3		3
Marketing							(2)	(2)
Commercial goods						(2)		(2)
Tax accounting							2	2
Vocational subjects Total	7	8	25	10	11(2)	14(2)	35(4)	35(4)

To have students experience, through experiments and practice, the basic techniques required in each industrial sector, increase their interest in and concern about the technology, and comprehend the various basic problems involved in industrial technology.

In other words, it involves practice which varies enormously from course to course. It is to be taken at the very beginning of the first year to give pupils a flavour of what is to come, be it using tools to make something or measuring or experimenting.

Industrial mathematics is taught in classrooms during the first year, and assumes no more than knowledge of third year junior high school mathematics. The textbook is common to all courses, but each mathematical principle is illustrated with a variety of alternative examples, so that teachers may pick and choose the relevant industrial setting for pupils with different specializations. Thus the machinery course pupils can concentrate on mechanics questions. The objective of industrial mathematics is to persuade pupils who do not necessarily enjoy academic maths of the need to use it in practical work contexts.

TEACHING AND ASSESSMENT OF PRACTICAL SUBJECTS

Practical subjects are, as everywhere, the most expensive subjects, but a variety of techniques are resorted to in order to keep costs down. Drawing and design are taught to whole classes of 40 pupils. The teacher gives a brief introduction and then the students work individually with the help of a textbook and the patrolling teacher. Pupils submit samples of their work to the teacher for assessment.

Other practical subjects involving experiments or the practice making of some object are taught to smaller groups — of 13–15 in the first two years, 10 in the third. Each group has a qualified teacher in attendance, and there are teaching assistants who prepare experiments, look after materials, clear up after the class, and also help the pupils. The usual organization is for groups to rotate around three or four units of practical work, each taking about 8 weeks, so that everyone gets to each unit in the course of a 35-week school year.

In principle there are no paper tests for such work. Pupils are instead assessed on:

1. A short report which they submit, describing the purpose, progress and final achievement of an experiment or trial manufacture.
2. Their behaviour in the classroom, with, for many of the

exercises, as much weight being put on co-operativeness as individual effort.
3. Attendance. The formal minimum to get credit is one-third of classroom hours.
4. The result of the practical exercise if there was an individual result.

Assessment methods vary from case to case. Measuring the ground in the architecture course may be assessed solely by a timed practical test. Or, an experiment may involve the whole group operating a single large piece of machinery — as in sanitation engineering. In that case each pupil would be allocated a different task and write a different report.

The end of term report gives an assessment of each pupil's performance in each subject on an unambiguous numerical scale — in some schools 1 to 5 as is standard in the lower school system, in others 1 to 10. The end of the year assessment determines whether a pupil can proceed to the next year. A very low mark even in one subject can lead to a pupil repeating a year, though this appears to be more common in practice in the schools which recruit from low down the ability range — often low morale schools with high drop-out rates. The drop-outs are often those who have been made to repeat a year.

EQUIPMENT AND MACHINERY FOR PRACTICE

There is great variation in the quality of schools' equipment. Since 1951 and the Industrial Education Promotion Law, the Ministry has set detailed standards for each course, and there has been a central Ministry fund to help schools to reach those standards. It provides one-third of any expenditure for such purposes to match the two-thirds put up — by the prefectural authorities in the case of public schools, by the owners in the case of private ones. About ¥8.5m of central government funds was available for this in 1985, implying a total expenditure of about 18 yen per student. (Annual capital grants for vocational school buildings run at about three times that figure.)

The equipment standards set, however, lag behind the changes in production technology; it would be surprising if they did not. Even at the above-average Kuramae school which has a 'practice factory' with a variety of lathes, all-purpose milling machines, NC milling machines, etc., most of the machines were over 10 years old. They are trying to update them, but some teachers hold that too much importance need not be given to machine vintage. The pursuit of the latest has more to do with pride and morale than with their real and necessary job — teaching the basics.

That argument does not apply to computers where obsolescence is so rapid. It is only recently that computer terminals have been acquired for whole-class teaching — 40 terminals and 20 printers. They are now provided on a five-year rental basis, and the manufacturers organize three-month training courses for teachers. There have also been efforts by prefectural governments to set up education centres which can apply for the Ministry subsidy mentioned earlier to purchase up-to-date equipment which is too expensive for individual schools — e.g., robots and mainframe computers. These centres have the dual purpose of providing facilities for pupils to practise and of running introductory and up-dating courses for teachers.

PRACTICAL WORK AT COMMERCIAL HIGH SCHOOLS

'Comprehensive practice', the practical subject common to all business-related courses, is taught in the second and third years. (Table 3.1b). It is basically a simulation of the business environment in the classroom. Each pupil plays the role of a shop, a wholesaler, a trading company, bank, a transport company, etc. to get practice in marketing, administration, clerical and accounting activities. Office machines are used where they can be afforded.

FORMAL QUALIFICATIONS

The school's own graduation certificate is the main goal of the vocational high school pupil, but he or she may also get an externally examined vocational certificate on the way. Chapter 7 describes Japan's system of skill tests in some detail. A number of the tests — those run by MITI and the Ministry of Labour as well as those on the approved list of the Ministry of Education — have preliminary grades which are specially intended for vocational high school students. Popular choices are the motor vehicle maintenance (third class) certificate, boiler technician certificate, the welding, electrician, dangerous chemical handler, pollution prevention supervisor's certificates for the industrial school pupils, and commercial English, typing, shorthand and book-keeping certificates for the commercial school pupils. Teachers encourage pupils to take these qualifications mainly to motivate them to learn, and to make them more confident in the value of what they have learned. There seems to be little thought that it would help them to get better jobs. Local employers (and the vast majority of vocational high school graduates seek work in local labour markets) are guided more by the school's reputation and their experience of employing past intakes when judging what skill levels they can expect. And beyond that they are more interested in personal qualities which they judge from interviews and teachers' reports.

COLLEGES OF TECHNOLOGY

The engineering world in Japan is less clearly stratified than in most other countries. (As a general principle, the Japanese go in for finely graded hierarchies in their organizations, rather than for broad stratal divisions.) Thus, there are two categories in common use — *ginosha*, craftsmen, and *gijutsusha* or *gijutsuya* (the latter when used in contrast to *jimuya*, non-technically qualified white-collar employees). The latter mean, basically, non-manual people on the technical side — whether high school or university graduates. (And, indeed, it does seem that transfer from high-school-graduate-scale jobs to university-graduate-scale jobs is easier on the technical than on the administrative side.)

Nevertheless, there was much discussion, in the 1950s and 1960s as high school graduation became the normal entry level for ginosha craftsmen, of the need for some intermediate level of training between ginosha level and full university level training. (When middle school had been providing the ginosha, vocational high schools were seen as playing that intermediate role.) A few junior colleges performed that function in a limited kind of way, but the junior college image was too specialized in its girls' finishing school role to attract good students. (Students on industrial courses at junior colleges were an eleven per cent minority in the mid-1960s and numbered only six per cent in 1980.)

The solution was a new kind of technical college recruiting at 15 and offering five-year courses in new well-equipped schools and with a heavy emphasis on new technologies. At present, as Table 1.1 shows, the 62 Colleges (54 of them national, 4 local government and 4 private) provide about 1 per cent of the entrants to the manufacturing labour force, enrolling over 9,500 boys and about 350 girls each year. They are well-equipped and at 12.5:1 have much better staffing ratios than either vocational high schools or universities. They offer courses

45

in all the main branches of engineering, and they have, now, a low drop-out rate. In total, over half of the course content over the five years is directly vocational, compared with only 44 per cent of a typical Technical High School. There is, however, a higher concentration on general subjects in the first two years of the course (82 per cent of the time in the first year, for example): it is in the last two years that the vocational training becomes more single-minded — 83–84 per cent of the timetable. The colleges also arrange work experience in a local factory — albeit a mere three-week summer assignment rather than a serious sandwich arrangement. It probably has more of a bearing on subsequent job finding than on the ability to absorb the curriculum content. (The heavy general course content in the early years meant that bright students tugged towards the general high-school-university route might be seduced into the colleges by the thought that they are not too definitively abandoning other options in their first two years.)

Even so, the colleges at first had trouble recruiting good students — or if they did recruit them, in retaining them beyond the age of 18 when the final choice between them and the alternative of a cram-school year followed by university had to be taken. Since none of the big companies which good students wanted to get into (see Table 2.6 for why) had salary scales for graduates of as yet non-existent schools, it represented a leap into the unknown, and an obviously inferior alternative to sticking to an academic-course high school and getting to a university engineering department.

The solution was the obvious one — making it possible to transfer to the third-year course of a four-year university. It would have required too much dilution of the vocational content of their five-year course to make this acceptable to most universities, so the alternative was adopted of setting up two new universities, at Nagaoka and Toyohashi for the express purpose of offering third- and fourth-year engineering courses to the graduates of Technical Colleges. These and other universities now take about 10 per cent of the graduates of the colleges. Although the majority of graduates go straight into industry, keeping open the possibility of progression to the university has considerably enhanced the colleges' attractiveness and increased, in consequence, the difficulty of getting into them. It will be recalled that in Iwaki it is students from the top 15 per cent of achievers who succeed in the all-prefecture competition for entry to the Fukushima College.

It is also relevant that a number of the larger companies have made special career provision for College of Technology graduates, creating a salary scale which puts them a cut above junior college graduates who have nominally the same number of years of full-time education. The Gumma College, one of the first to be founded in 1962, recently traced a sample of 1,300 of its graduates. A quarter of those now aged 35–39 were in managerial positions, but primarily in smaller companies. As compared with a similar survey five years earlier, the proportion who were shop floor workers had declined 'considerably' and the proportion engaged in research, development and design had gone up (this, the report did specify) from 22 to 34 per cent (*Nihon Kogyo Shimbun*, 8 Sept. 1986).

JUNIOR COLLEGES

As already mentioned, junior colleges suffer a good deal from the girls' finishing school image — and indeed 90 per cent of their students are female. The single vocational stream of any significance is the education course through which it is possible to qualify as a primary school teacher. There are also courses for auxiliary health workers and day-care centre workers. Altogether there are about 120,000 students on vocational courses in 1985, about a third of the total enrolment in junior colleges. It has to be said, however, that many of these vocational certificates are used to enhance marriage chances (and to become 'good education-crazy mums' [Kyoiku-mama]) rather than to find jobs. It is the special training schools rather than the junior colleges which train most of the nurses and play-school teachers, for instance.

UNIVERSITIES

Table 3.2 shows the proportions of four-year university students on various kinds of explicitly vocational courses. Those proportions have been quite stable over the last two decades. Engineering increased its weighting considerably in the first half of the 1960s — from 15 to 20 per cent — and has remained stable since — a considerable achievement considering the near-doubling of total enrolments. Medicine has long since taken about 2 per cent of entrants. Agriculture — today the first choice of only a minority of the students who take it — took 4.7 per cent in 1960 and still took 3.5 per cent in 1985. Institutional inertia is a Japanese problem, too, though there has been some change in content — addition of ecology specializations, for example.

47

Table 3.2 Distribution of university students by course

	1960 %	1970 %	1985 %
Science	2.7	3.1	3.4
Engineering	15.4	21.1	19.8
Agriculture	4.7	3.7	3.5
Medicine : Dentistry	3.8	2.8	4.3
Other medical-related	2.1	2.1	2.5
Merchant shipping	0.2	0.1	0.1
Home economics	1.4	1.7	1.9
Education	10.5	6.9	7.8
Other*	59.2	58.4	56.8
Total	601,464	1,344,358	1,734,392

Source: Mombu-tokei, 1986
* Other includes arts, humanities and social sciences.
N.B. *Percentages may not add up to 100.0 due to rounding.*

There is, of course, a big range in 'quality' in the vocational as well as in the general educational courses. A ranking of universities by their contributions to research and graduate teaching shows that the higher the rank of the university, the higher the proportion of engineering students, but engineering education is far from being confined to research-oriented universities (Amano 1984). Table 2.5, it will be recalled, showed another attempted ranking of science and engineering courses, compared with economics courses, using the scholastic ability score (hensachi) calculated to be necessary to get into each faculty.

It will be apparent from that table, first, that not all the 70,000-plus science and engineering graduates of Japanese universities are intellectual high-flyers, though, secondly, that they contain a higher proportion of high-ability students than the approximately equal numbers taking economics and business studies. The (reputedly rather small) direct vocational relevance of economics courses and the (only slightly greater) relevance of business studies courses is a worthy study in its own right. It is one on which we have little material, however, and we here concentrate on the much more commonly discussed engineering and science courses.

Engineering is found in both public and private universities. As Table 2.5 makes clear public universities have a high proportion of the best students, but there is a considerable spill-over tail of private institutions which recruit students of ability levels (relative to population averages) which might be considered marginal for degree courses at British polytechnics (though their entry achievement levels may well be higher).

As at other levels of education, there is a quite high degree of central control by the Ministry of Education. There are, first, framework regulations which set a pattern to which all degree courses must conform. The award of a degree requires satisfactory performance in courses totalling 124 units, of which so many must be in foreign languages, so many in physical education (even for the not-so open university, the University of the Air), and so on, though universities can vary the framework if they insist. Nagoya University teaches only one foreign language for example, and there is a good deal of local variation in practice — final year projects, for example, may be given a much higher weighting than their ostensible unit value would suggest. Nevertheless it is still the case that the framework rules require the first two years of the four-year course to be devoted to general education subjects, similar in content for all students irrespective of their intending specialization.

Only the last two years of the course are devoted to study in the chosen specialty. Here there is a good deal more scope for local initiative (and the two sample curricula in Fig. 3.1 show something of the range of variation in the teaching of electrical engineering.) Even here, however, in the public universities where the bulk of the best engineering teaching is concentrated, central control compounds academic conservatism in slowing the response of universities to new developments in scientific knowledge and industrial practice. The slowness of shifts in the distribution of engineering faculty by field has recently been analysed as an index of universities' inability to respond to change (Tsukahara and Muto 1986). Go-ahead professors can and do provide new courses, but the emergence of an important new subject — opt-electronics or laser semi-conductors, for instance — requires the establishment of a new 'chair' (koza, meaning literally something like 'lecture-hall unit', and involving, usually, a professorship, one or two supporting lectureships and an equipment budget), though there is an increasing tendency towards a departmental system which allows the reallocation of individual posts to new fields. Either way a major new department may take several years of negotiation, particularly in the last decade of budgetary stringency, and it may well be that new creations are at the expense of established posts — a process which has led to a decline in the number of bottom-of-the-ladder assistantships, a matter of some concern to a government committee which looked recently at problems of research manpower (Dore 1986).

Figure 3.1 Sample curricula of university engineering faculties, 1986

(a) Osaka University, Tokyo Institute of Technology, etc.

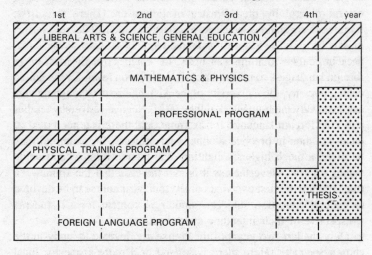

(b) University of Tokyo (Department of Electrical and Electronic Engineering)

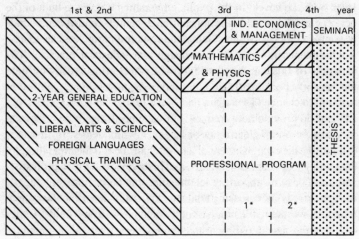

streaming: 1 : Electronic Circuits or Power
2* : Devices, Information Theory or Power

Source: Po. S. Chung, 'Engineering education systems in Japanese universities', *Comparative Education* 30, iii, August 1986

The private universities can respond more rapidly. They too are under the jurisdiction of a Ministry of Education Council which controls the grant of the title of university and the accompanying tax advantages. Its work, however, is largely concentrated on the initial vetting of eligibility, and its monitoring role very largely reduced to mere notification requirements.

The broad base of the first two university years does ensure that the universities do not produce 'narrow engineers'. The concentration on professional subjects in the last two years does seem to be close, however; there are rarely any business-related courses in engineering faculties, for example. There seems, also, to be rather less practical work than in most countries and a greater reliance on one-way lectures than on dialogue or discussion — which, reputedly, the deferential non-inquisitiveness of the typical Japanese student makes it difficult to get going. Assessment varies, depending on the teacher of each course, but is usually by a mixture of end-tests and course-work. A four-grade, 'excellent', 'good', 'pass', 'fail' marking is usually used for individual courses, but these marks are not aggregated in any way and degrees are pass/fail — or rather, pass/awaiting completion of requirements, or pass/withdrawn; the degree depends on the accumulation of unit credits. Overall failure rates are low ('Hard to get into, easy to come out of' is what the Japanese say about their universities, but individual course failures are common. Twenty-five per cent of students on any one course are likely to be repeaters, and over twenty per cent take five years, not four to graduate.)

One reason for low failure rates — one reason why one would expect failure rates to be lower however strict the examination procedure — is because of the homogeneity of student intakes, which is much greater in Japan than in most other countries for two reasons; first because of the centralized uniformity of the school system: secondly because of the ability-homogenising effect of the entrance examination 'slicing system'. This has a considerable importance for the standards attained, particularly, as Kinmouth notes in his comparison of a Kobe and a California engineering department, in mathematics. A lot of the initial general maths is in Japan a quick refresher course. In California, for some students, it has to be lengthy and remedial (Kinmouth 1986).

Whether low failure rates have anything to do with it or not, Japanese universities seem not, in anybody's estimation, to be high-pressure institutions. It is frequently said that the four years of university life represent the 'moratorium period' in the Japanese middle-class male life cycle. Employers' recruitment decisions are

51

more influenced by the 'ability-label' which university entrance confers than by any evidence of above-average performance at the university. Hence the incentives for study beyond the minimum required for satisfactory passes are small. Hence university students find it easy to get by on a few hours' study a week, borrowing from studious friends or buying in second-hand book shops notes on unattended lectures to get through end-of-term exams, and can devote the rest of their time to earning money in part-time jobs and spending it on consumerist recreation. (*Manga* [cartoon books] and *mah-jong* being the archetypal forms of student recreations according to those who deplore the trend.) But even those who deplore the trend find it understandable; after a workaholic adolescence devoted to securing the best university label they can manage, and with a workaholic life in their chosen company ahead of them, it is not unreasonable to try to enjoy the interval.

This generalization about university students does not necessarily apply to engineering students, however, for at least two reasons. The first applies to the students at the top end of the ability/quality spectrum, in the universities which have graduate schools. Science and engineering are the only branches of study in which graduate schools have developed for reasons other than apprentice training for the academic profession or to provide a haven for those who want to postpone choice of a career. Engineering masters degrees *do* confer a career advantage, and do so increasingly as knowledge becomes more specialized and the R & D establishments of Japanese firms which look for masters and PhDs expand. Hence, competition to get into a master's course can be keen, especially at the top universities where master's courses typically take 50 per cent of the undergraduate intake (and the doctoral course 25 per cent) so that chances of success are high enough to make progression to graduate school the dominant ambition of students.

The other reason is related, but applies at the other end of the spectrum. In the vocational subjects of engineering and science, employers are more interested in substantive learning accomplishments and less predominantly influenced by the university-rank ability-labelling effect than when recruiting arts or social studies graduates. (That is precisely why graduate education has taken off in Japan only in science and engineering.) Moreover, the students at the lesser private provincial engineering colleges cannot look forward to a protected seniority-waged career in a large corporation. They are more likely destined for a local small or medium firm in which their career is going to depend on their real ability; they have a stronger incentive to make sure that they really do learn to cope.

If it is true that, in a Japanese engineering education, for the most part formal instruction is as 'deadly dull' as writers like Kinmouth say it is, there seems to be some considerable redemption to be found in the graduating thesis. This usually accounts for a third or more of the unit requirements of the final year. For the purpose of this thesis students become integrated members of a real research community, one of a dozen or so students admitted to a professor's personal 'lab', his *Kenkyushitsu*. At its best this can be a valuable and intellectually exciting experience of hands-on research apprenticeship. At the very least, it provides occasion for independent inquiry, for learning how to find out what is the state of the art in any field — and usually for handling foreign (mostly English) language sources.

UNIVERSITY-INDUSTRY LIAISON

One other thing on which most observers seem to agree is that a Japanese engineering education is rather more theoretical than practical, and leans more towards basic science than is common in Britain or the United States. It seems also to be true that the research conducted in Japanese engineering departments is closer to the basic/fundamental than to the commercializable/developmental end of the spectrum than research in their British counterparts.

This is symptomatic of the fact that the university-industry relationship is a good deal more distant than in Britain. The feeling that the citadels of disinterested scholarship should not be corrupted by those who live in the world of the profit motive is a strong one, and one which in the public universities is embodied in regulations which greatly restrict professorial consultancies or the receipt of research contracts. Private universities are less formally restricted, but they do not contain the high-prestige faculties, and tend to follow the lead of their public university colleagues. As MITI is frequently wont to deplore, Japanese corporations commission more research from universities in the US and Europe than from universities in Japan. If Grayson's count is correct and there are about 800 Japanese students in US science and engineering graduate schools (Grayson 1983b:145), that may well mean that there are more Japanese company-sponsored graduate students overseas than in Japanese universities. Company sponsorship of undergraduate students sometimes happens, but is rare and informal; the universities do not encourage it or seek to formalize it. (There has been considerable change in this respect and an increase in research contracting since 1985.)

53

Companies are, of course, keen to compete for good students and expend considerable effort in doing so, but their favourite method is reliance on professorial recommendation rather than by open 'milk-round' invitation. For these purposes firms do cultivate close relations with professors of science and engineering, as with professors of other subjects, and encourage their former students to keep in touch with them. And, certainly, the fact that a personnel department cultivates a professor in order to stake a claim to his best students, and that the firm contains a number of his ex-students, increases the likelihood that the research department might seek his co-operation in research, or send employees to him for graduate work — though not very much.

The recently heightened concern in Japan with scientific creativity and the need for Japanese industry to move a little further towards the basic end of the basic research/applied research/development continuum, has brought a renewed concern with industry-university collaboration (Dore 1986). Several special programmes of the Science and Technology Agency and MITI are designed to promote research collaboration (with — usually grudging and limited — support from the Ministry of Education). But about the educational role of universities there seems to be relatively little dissatisfaction. Kinmouth puts it well:

> Japanese companies do not expect engineering graduates to possess substantial mechanical skills on graduation . . . Since the early 1960s there has been no pressure from corporations to make Japanese engineering education more explicitly practical. Moreover, in recent years, the non-vocational, non-specialized (relative to the United States) bent in Japanese education has come to be seen as a strength.
>
> In volatile markets, firms can only guess at future needs when they hire . . . flexibility is more important than immediately applicable mechanical skills. Studies of Japanese engineers show that within 2–3 years of hiring more than 40 per cent will be following a technical specialty substantially different from that which they studied in college. This is coupled to a strong corporate sense that narrow specialization would work against success in such promising areas as 'mechatronics', . . . fine ceramics, fiber optics and so on.
>
> (Kinmouth 1986:411)

OVERALL STANDARDS

Given these differences, as between Japan and, say, Britain, in what is expected of universities, and given the difference that Japan acknowledges and Britain (with its systems of external examining, etc.) does not acknowledge, wide differences of quality between universities, it is, as Rawle remarked in his GEC study after investigating the matter over some months in Japan, 'difficult to come to any objective assessment of the standard of Japanese university science and engineering courses.' He quotes a Japanese who had taught and worked in the US as saying that general standards were similar in the two countries 'with the Japanese having possibly a slight edge in specialized knowledge while the Americans had an advantage in the breadth of their education,' while at the same time the Japanese were more 'bookish'. As for Britain, it is 'reasonable to suggest that the Japanese graduate at B.Sc./B.Eng. level is a less knowledgeable engineer than his British counterpart. At M.Sc./M.Eng. level there is probably little difference' (Rawle 1983:32).

4

Post-secondary, non-university VET: public sector

For a country so full of comprehensive reference books regarding everything educational, it is surprisingly difficult to get a comprehensive view of the public provision of post-secondary VET, largely because of the jealous sectionalism of the several smaller ministries which sponsor various types of schools and colleges. Table 4.1, for instance, which has Ministry of Education statistics for those post-secondary non-university VET institutions which enjoy the legal status of *Senshu-gakko* (Special Training Schools) or *Kakushu-gakko*

Table 4.1 Post-secondary, non-university vocational schools and colleges: types, schools and pupils

Types of school & numbers of pupils	1976	1980	1984
Senshu-gakko			
Public Schools	74	333	348
Their Pupils	8,122	36,471	41,313
Private Schools	820	2,187	2,587
Their Pupils	123,367	396,443	494,944
Sub-total Schools	894	2,520	2,935
Sub-total Pupils	131,489	432,914	536,257
Kakushu-gakko			
Public Schools	275	169	130
Their Pupils	22,389	13,307	10,040
Private Schools	6,730	5,137	4,346
Their Pupils	1,064,748	711,077	570,020
Sub-total Schools	7,005	5,306	4,476
Sub-total Pupils	1,087,137	724,384	580,060
Total Schools	7,899	7,823	7,311
Total Pupils	1,218,504	1,157,298	1,116,317

Source: Senshu, 1986

Miscellaneous Schools) grossly underrepresents the public sector. It does not, for instance, include any of the network of craft and technician training schools run by the Ministry of Labour. A major reason seems to be that the Ministry of Education exercises loose supervisory powers over *senshu* and *kakushu* schools, and no Ministry of Labour bureaucrat is going to submit his schools to any kind of jurisdiction of the Minister of Education. On the other hand, many of the schools attached to national hospitals run by the Ministry of Health — for nurses, physiotherapists, rehabilitation workers with the blind, etc. — have been allowed or encouraged to claim Senshu status.

The best way to describe these public sector schools, therefore, is Ministry system by Ministry system. We begin with the largest and most important network, that run by the Ministry of Labour.

MINISTRY OF LABOUR SCHOOLS

It is not a very extensive system. It can cater for initial training, for about 31,000 entrants a year, or 1½ per cent of a recent age group. Its cost, at about £250 m., supplemented by perhaps another £30 m. from prefectural funds, represents about two-thirds of the Ministry's total training budget. (See Table 4.2.) Its outline shape is as follows:

The base level consists of 217 Vocational Training Schools run by prefectural authorities, and another two run by city authorities, according to the specifications of, and with 50 per cent funding from, the Ministry.

Then there are 80 Comprehensive Vocational Training Schools run by the Employment Promotion Projects Corporation — a creature of the Ministry financed partly out of the fund originally set up to use oil taxes to deal with the 1960s run down of the coal industry, but recently primarily by the Workers' Insurance Fund.

For the handicapped, there are 18 special schools.

For training vocational trainers there are 11 junior colleges and one four-year 'university college' which is also a centre for research, curriculum development and textbook production. (It is called a *daigakko* rather than *daigaku*. The Ministry of Education would not allow the title 'university' to any mere creature of another ministry.) It offers a basic four-year training course to some 240 students a year (for teachers at Vocational Training Schools), six-month courses in training skills for about 100 people a year on

Table 4.2 Ministry of Labour training budget, 1986

	(¥ millions; ¥ 1m = £4,500)	
	Expenditure	Difference from 1985
1. Fostering the 'learning enterprise', through encouragement of enterprise training efforts	12,349	+ 5.8%
Expenses of coordinating bodies, councils, conferences, courses for trainers	1,629	
Expansion of Service Centre	122	
Grants to employers to support training activities	8,597	
Development of training centres to promote special local needs	2,000	
2. Grants to employers to subsidise their encouragement of employees' self-development	783	+ 50.6%
3. Promotion of skill development through public sector institutions	65,517	+ 5.2%
Prefectural Vocational Training Centres	7,692	
Higher Vocational Training Centres, Colleges, Universities	45,275	
Retraining programmes for redundant workers	5,468	
Grants and loans to students	2,775	
Collaboration with private sector training establishments	1,385	
Quality upgrading for private sector trainers	2,886	
4. Special programmes to cope with technical change and the ageing of society	2,148	+ 28.8%
Micro-electronics-related	1,222	
Computer-aided instruction	4	
Other new technology-related	694	
Training programmes for the elderly	227	

5. Programmes for the handicapped and others needing special caring attention	5,059	+15.7%
6. Maintenance of the skill testing system	748	−8.6%
Central expenditure and subsidies to prefectures for skill-testing system	667	
Promotion of within-enterprise skill test systems	13	
Encouragement of a respect for skill: medals, competitions, skill Olympics (final year)	67	
7. Overseas aid in the training field to developing countries	1,266	+15.6%
8. Adjustment of the administrative structure for skill training	347	+13.3%
Total expenditure	88,216	+6.6%
Sources of revenue		
1. General budget	10,773	−22.2%
2. Workers insurance fund special account	77,376	+12.4%
3. Oil import tax special fund	66	+0.2%
4. (Loan finance)	200	0.0%
Total revenue	88,415	+6.6%

Source: Rodosho, Shokugyo noryoku kaihatsu kyoku (Ministry of Labour, Vocational Skill Development Bureau), *Shokugyo noryoku kaihatsukyoku shuyo yosan(an) no gaiyo* (Outline of major budget items in the Bureau's 1986 budget)

secondment from firms, and a variety of shorter up-grading courses for trainers both from industry and from training schools.

(See Cantor 1984)

The system was built up in the 1950s. It belonged to and suited the 1950s and 1960s when 15-year-old middle school leavers still made up the majority of new labour market entrants (see Table 1.1). It did not cater, even then, to the most able of those 15-year-olds — they were snapped up by the recruiters from the rapidly expanding large firms which were prepared to give them an on-the-job training suited to their own particular needs. But they offered for those in the next band of the ability spectrum (or for those who might have got such a job, but did not want to leave home for an enterprise dormitory), the opportunity to get a basic-skill training in a variety of industrial crafts, and thereby substantially to improve their attractiveness to employers or their contribution to the family business (nearly a quarter of Japan's non-agricultural workers were self-employed or family workers in 1965, and over one-fifth still are so today).

But rapidly the catchment pool of 15-year-old school leavers dwindled from 50 to its present 5 per cent of the age group. Simultaneously, the demand for traditional engineering skills declined. The Ministry schools were slow to adapt. New courses meant not new staff, but retraining of their existing, lifetime-employed, teachers who were not always up to the task — having had little industrial experience anyway, and not much chance of getting any. They were slow to develop courses for the new potential markets in office and electronic skills suitable for the 18-year-olds who, though in relative terms from the same segment of the ability spectrum as their original clientele (that is to say those who neither proceed to university nor manage to get lifetime-prospect jobs with large firms) nevertheless have better developed abilities and higher pretensions. The gap was filled by private-sector provision on the scale indicated in Table 4.1. Meanwhile the Ministry of Labour schools declined in prestige and importance.

Perhaps the best idea of scope and coverage can be given by describing the provision in Fukushima prefecture, a north-eastern prefecture with about two million inhabitants, rather more rural than average (agriculture and manufacturing each claim about a quarter of a million workers, though the farm workers are, of course, much more part-time and semi-retired than the industrial workers). Per capita income is about 17 per cent below the national average.

There are vocational training schools in six of the prefecture's towns. The largest one, in Koriyama (300,000 inhabitants) for instance, has 70 places for high school graduates on one-year electrician courses and filled 56 of them in 1986. Its car mechanic two-year course had 20 places — also for high school graduates — and admitted 22. Two one-year courses in architecture and architectural drawing drew only 27 high-school leavers for 40 places.

Then there are three of the original courses for 15-year-olds — in welding, building and painting. They slightly over-filled their 75 places, though three of the welders and three of the painters were over 30 and were admitted under the support-for-retraining provisions.

The other schools have much the same pattern, but with some variation in the nature of the courses. Dress-making, sheet-metal fabrication, plastering, stone-masonry, woodwork and sewing complete the list of courses on offer. Most of them lead to, and are based on the curriculum for, the vocational skill tests which will be described in Chapter 7.

Fukushima has three of the nation's centrally-funded Comprehensive Vocational Training Schools. Their courses are not much different from those of the prefectural schools; they are, in fact, more predominantly concerned with courses for 15-year-old leavers than the latter. What is distinctive about these schools, however, is that they double up as retraining centres. One of them, for instance, in an area where the last remaining coal mines are closing, has filled 20–30 places in 1986 for each of eight one-year courses in welding, sheet-metal fabrication, electrical installation, painting, building, plastering, plumbing and printing.

Completion rates overall, in the whole nine Fukushima schools, were 82 per cent, on a total 1985 intake of 657 students chosen from 999 applicants for 755 places. Or, rather, 999 applications; those who applied for a more popular course but settled for a less popular one would be counted at least twice, so that overall (recorded) demand hardly exceeds supply.

These schools, especially the two biggest in the two main towns, also put on special short weekend courses — on computer database systems (12 hours over 2 days), on arc-welding with special attention to safety (three days, 21 hours), lathe work (12 weekend hours: bring own cutting tools and materials: practice on an Ikegai ED18), etc. Some are for personal interest like the calligraphy course and the owners' car maintenance course, but of the 48 courses offered in 1986 at the main Fukushima Comprehensive Vocational Training School, 19 were (like the lathe course just mentioned) refresher courses for

61

those taking national skill tests. These courses are assigned a very small part of the overall prefectural budget — less than one per cent — but that is because the staff time is not costed against them. At the Fukushima school they absorbed a full 150 man-days of teaching — and presumably rather more of preparation — for the 35-man staff. (By agreement with the union, staff get time-and-a-half days off in the week in compensation for this weekend teaching.)

The scale of operations in Fukushima was about typical of the whole country — enrolment per million inhabitants was, in fact, about 50 per cent above average. Nationally, it appears that nearly a half of the entrants to the courses are still drawn from the five per cent of the age group who leave the regular school system at the age of 15; 27 per cent were just out of high school and the remaining quarter — predominantly high school graduates — had been out of school for some time. The three most popular types of course — the only ones to enroll a thousand students nationally each year — are in automobile mechanics, building and metal-working machinery.

A few schools have impressive banks of computers and the odd, rather dated NC machine, but the equipment is not in general impressive. The teaching, however, is said to be proficient and meticulous, and the standards of competence reached are respectable.

MINISTRY OF HEALTH NURSING SCHOOLS

Schools of nursing fall under the jurisdiction of the Ministry of Health. There are several routes to a nursing qualification. Once, one of the most popular was that which began at the age of 15 after middle school, and led, after a two-year course or a three-year part-time course, to the qualification of auxiliary nurse — a prefectural qualification — which then could be transformed, after three years' practical experience and a two-year course of further study, into a full national nursing certificate. Once a flood, girls following this route amount now to a mere trickle, thanks to the spread of high school attendance, though the auxiliary nursing certificate remains of some importance because of the development of nursing courses within regular vocational high schools. There are over 130 such schools now, and the auxiliary certificate can be obtained there — and followed directly, if desired, with the two-year topping-up course leading to a full national nursing certificate without the requirement of three years' practical experience. There are still 188,000 auxiliary nurses in Japan, compared with 252,000 full nurses (four per cent of the former and two per cent of the latter being men.)

The standard route now, however, is to complete high school and then to take a three-year course at a nursing school at the end of which the national examination may be taken. There are also ten university departments with four-year nursing courses leading to the same qualification and much the same training, but accompanying it with more general education, thereby conferring higher prestige, the possibility of higher salaries, and increased probability of marrying a doctor.

These schools are as varied in their ownership and constitution as the hospitals to which they are attached. On the island of Hokkaido, for instance, there are twenty-seven schools, five attached to national hospitals run directly by the Ministry of Health, three run by the prefectural government, ten by city administrations, four by the Japan Red Cross, and the remainder by the Workers Welfare Fund and other similar bodies.

The curriculum is similar, however, in all 423 such schools throughout the country, and the Ministry of Health which is the licensing authority lays down the appropriate division of hours over the three years. There are to be 390 hours out of a 3,375 total devoted to general education, a third of them to English; 30 hours each for physics, chemistry, biology, statistics, sociology, psychology and education, and double that number for physical education. The specialist work divides: 885 classroom hours and 1,770 hours of practical work, allocated as shown in Table 4.3.

A similar pattern is repeated for the wide variety of other health-related qualifications. There are state examinations for health visitors and midwives, each of which requires a six-month course beyond the nursing certificate. All of the certificates for physiotherapists, occupational therapists, eyesight therapists, radiographers, pathology lab technicians, etc. which require three-year courses, or for dental technicians and dental hygienists for which there are two-year courses, are national certificates with a national certifying examination. Courses are given at national schools (attached to Ministry of Health hospitals), public (prefectural and city) schools, and at private *senshu-gakko* or *kakushu-gakko*. The national institutions are cheaper. Their state blessing in itself gives them higher prestige. Their cheapness and prestige make them attractive; they can therefore be selective in their admissions: their good students then attract the best doctors and teachers who attract the best facilities — which further enhances their attractions to students, which further increases selectivity, which itself enhances their prestige and increases their attractiveness to staff, their

Table 4.3 Curriculum of nurse training course

Subject	Number of hours	
	Classroom	Practical
General education	390	
General medical	330	
Introduction to medicine	15	
Anatomy	45	
Physiology	45	
Biochemistry (including diets)	45	
Pharmacology	30	
Pathology	45	
Microbiology	45	
Public Health	30	
Social Welfare	15	
Health legislation	15	
Nursing	885	1,905
Introduction to nursing	60	
Nursing skills	90	90
General practical		180
Nursing adults: introduction	30	
Adult preventive medicine	60	
Nursing for:		
Internal complaints	135	435
Mental illness	30	90
Surgical treatments	90	330
Orthopaedic surgery	45	90
Skin diseases	15	20
Urinary complaints	15	25
Gynaecological complaints	30	45
Eye complaints	15	15
ENT complaints	15	15
Dental complaints	15	15
Health clinic practice		45
Paediatric nursing	120	300
Maternity nursing	120	210
Total	1,605	1,905

ability to be choosy about their staff, hence that staff's substantive quality, hence their attractiveness to students . . . .

And so the prestige gradient, once established, gets steeper. If you are living in Hiroshima, for instance, and want to be a dental hygienist or a dental technician, you can try to become one of the twenty-year-olds admitted annually to each course at the dental department of Hiroshima (national) university hospital. The annual fee is about £160. The entrance examination covers English, calculus, general science, physics or chemistry, Japanese language and literature, and drawing and sculpting for technicians. Hygienists can offer biology instead of physics or chemistry and do not need to sculpt.

For the unlucky who are not among the top twenty on either exam list, but still want to be dental hygienists, admission is easier (the entrance examination itself requires no maths and only biology among the sciences) at the Hiroshima Dental College (founded 1957 by the Hiroshima Medical Association). But first-year fees are £2,000 with an extra £700 for the cost of materials used in practicals. Would-be dental technicians can go to the Hiroshima College of Dental Technology (where they are required to sketch and sculpt in the entrance exam, but not to do maths) and charged no less than £5,000 for the first year (payable in installments: dormitory fees extra for female students from out of town). It is fairly safe to say that every one of the students at these private schools would have preferred to be in the state school if they had managed to secure admission.

In some other towns there is an intermediate opportunity ranking between the national and the private. Some of the nation's 90-plus dental hygiene schools and 70-plus dental technician schools are prefectural and city establishments. They are intermediate in fees (though usually closer to state levels), intermediate in difficulty of entry, and intermediate in prestige.

The basic pattern just described is, of course, a pervasive one in Japan's meritocracy, at the high school and university level as well as in the vocational field.

OTHER CENTRAL GOVERNMENT PROVISION

Other ministries also run schools. There are eight seamen's schools, for instance, run by the Ministry of Transport, the first set up in 1939. Some of these still take 15-year-olds for three-year courses, but the majority of their students are now high school graduates on one-year courses — either in general seamanship or on the ship's cook or ship's purser courses. The curriculum of these schools has recently been thoroughly revamped to cope with changes in shipping technology. There are also shipping and fisheries courses in some fifty regular (Education Ministry) vocational high schools, of course. For officer training, there are four marine universities (two of them public) and two other universities with marine departments, as well as five special training schools with 2–3 year courses in marine engineering, telecommunications, etc., also run by the Ministry. Needless to say, as the seaman is rapidly automated out of existence, this is not an area into which one can attract students at high fees. A year's course at the seamen's schools costs only £1,800 including full board, and scholarships of up to £700 are available from a special seamen's fund.

LOCAL GOVERNMENT

Local governments — of prefectures and cities — are by no means inactive in the educational field, but their efforts do seem largely to be circumscribed by central government initiative. That is to say, they provide, as was suggested earlier apropos of the dental schools, public provision additional to that provided by the state network, but within the same framework, to the same standards, and usually in a field where (expensive) private provision is also available. It is rare for local authorities to take any genuinely innovative initiative. One looks in vain, for instance, through the list of computer and business schools for any run by local authorities.

PUBLIC CORPORATIONS, THE SERVICES

Major contributions to the nation's pool of skills are also made, of course, by the initial training programmes offered to new recruits by the armed forces, the coastguard service, the now-privatised NTT, the national railways, etc. With lifetime employment, private sector industry reaps less benefit from these efforts than in most countries.

5

Private sector, non-university training schools

The newspapers frequently carry comments about the rapid growth of the *senshu-gakko*, usually translated as special training schools, and there is no doubt that the number of such schools has steadily increased since the category was created in 1976. Table 4.1 shows, however, that over the last ten years, the total number of students in the two types of schools — *senshu* and the pre-existing category of *kakushu* or 'miscellaneous' schools — has been fairly constant; in fact shown a slight decline. What seems to have been happening is a steady process of transformation of kakushu schools into the 'higher' category of senshu schools, though there have, also, been substantial changes of substance — a further decline in courses for 15-year-olds rather than 18-year-olds; an increase in girls' vocational training for employment (design, journalism, etc.) rather than (the old dress-making courses) for wifehood, an increase in technical courses, especially with information industries.

There are, also, recorded in no statistics, a number of non-recognised schools which fall into neither category, but may nevertheless appear in some of the training school guides. The Japan Grooming School, for example, which can take you over a two-year course to a Beginners' Class Trimmer's Licence for the All-Japan Association for the Guidance of Dog-lover Technicians as well as teaching you about running pet salons (charge £3,000 per annum) *is* registered as a kakushu school, but neither the Sepia Pet Care School, nor the Bow-wow Beauty University (also £3,000) in other, equally salubrious, suburbs of Tokyo have acquired that status.

There are tax advantages in being registered either as a kakushu or as a senshu school, and the more stringent requirements for senshu registration since the 1976 law created the category mean that there are also prestige advantages in being a senshu school.

The main differences are: senshu courses must last for at least a year, whereas the kakushu schools can also offer three-month courses; a year's senshu tuition must cover at least 800 hours (450 hours for evening courses) whereas a kakushu school needs only 680. Senshu schools need university graduates to teach high-school leavers, and half of them have to be full-time, whereas anybody can teach at a kakushu school. Other conditions concern size of classroom (three square metres per senshu pupil, only 2.31 per kakushu pupil), minimum numbers of pupils, pupil-teacher ratios, etc.

TYPES OF SCHOOL

Some idea of the range, the flavour and the promise of these schools can be derived from leafing through the full-page advertisements which fill the first quarter-inch of a two-inch-thick guide to these schools (Senshu 1986). A bakery (one-year) and general cake-maker's (three-year) school shows a photograph of its new three-storey premises in central Tokyo, miraculously shorn of all surrounding buildings, and advertises itself as laying a foundation stone for the twenty-first century. ('Créer c'est notre plaisir.') The Kanda Foreign Language Institute takes over a thousand pupils for practical English and English typing. The 'only recognized Jewellery Technical College in Tokyo' has a striking picture of a girl's foot with a large decorative stone attached to the ankle and the caption, 'You have to be in love with them'. A more sober architectural school has a page full of business-like details of the dozen daytime, ten night-time and six correspondence courses (architectural design, building equipment, surveying, interior co-ordination, etc.) and the caption, 'The enthusiasm of youth: stake it on a hard skill'. An animation school offers a free try-out day on the last Sunday of every month for those thinking of taking its one-year or two-year courses. ('Practical teaching by front-rank practitioners: 100% job placements as our goal, and in 1984 our achievement.') A medical school has courses for dieticians and clinical test technicians, a business school offers one-year courses for secretaries, for electronic calculator operators and for 'OA instructors' capable of handling all aspects of office automation. It claims to teach *man-tsu-man* — i.e., in classes of not more than ten. And so on.

Overall the distribution of the half-million-plus students in these schools as between types of courses was, in 1985, as follows (Senshu 1986: 46). Three-quarters of the students were on courses which required high-school graduation. The rest were also largely populated by high school graduates, though they could be entered at the age of 15, and the Ministry has recently recognized some twenty schools with three-year courses as conferring the same educational status as high school graduation.

	%
Industrial	18.7
Agricultural	0.1
Medical	24.5
Services affected by sanitary regulations	
(barbers, restaurants, etc.)	9.4
Education, social welfare	2.8
Commerce	12.5
Domestic science	14.9
Arts, design, media, etc.	17.1
	100.0

Who gets to these schools? Researchers at the National Institute for Educational Research have done a detailed study of the 1983 progression rates from about a thousand high schools (Iwaki and Mimizuka 1986). First, graduates of high school general courses were nearly twice as likely to end up in senshu schools as graduates from vocational courses. Secondly, the researchers looked at senshu entrance by high school 'rank'. They divided their schools into the high-achiever schools from which more than 80 per cent proceed to a college or university (14 per cent of the total), secondly, those from which 60–80 per cent proceed to a university, and so on to the fifth category — nearly half the total — the 'work stream' schools from which less than 20 per cent entered a university. They found that the highest percentage of entrants to senshu-gakko (20 per cent of all leavers) comes in the fourth category — schools where 20–40 per cent of leavers went on to college or university. Those in higher ranks are less likely to go because they are bent on getting into colleges or universities — though the contraction in university places has been raising senshu entrance rates over time from among the graduates of those schools too. Those at the bottom are less likely to go because they have long since been mentally prepared to go straight to work at the end of high school; 'the system' long since made it clear that the university was not for them — though, again, time series show that a restriction in job opportunities leads to an increase in numbers going on to senshu-gakko from these schools too. But the prime candidates for senshu entry are those in the intermediate-rank schools, where environmental pressures keep them wavering between trying for a job or getting further training.

The researchers uncovered, also, a geographical locational effect as well as a school effect. Some prefectures have far cheaper senshu places available than others. Higher overall prefectural attendance rates at such schools leads to a greater salience of senshu schools in the public consciousness, which increases the propensity to consider that option. And so on. Thus, even schools with the same level of university progression have different senshu entry rates depending on the prefecture. The 20–40 per cent schools which have an overall 20 per cent senshu entry rate, have a 27 per cent rate in the most senshu-entry-prone prefectures, a 17 per cent rate in the least.

But quite clearly, as other studies show, 'opting for a senshu school' is not by any means a single homogeneous category of action. It is frequently suggested that the senshu schools are filled with what are known as the 'might-as-well' tribe. Disappointed in their initial hopes of passing the entrance test for a good firm, or the college or university they had hoped for, they decide that they 'might as well' try a senshu-gakko in the hope that it might improve their job chances.

But there are other different categories. There *are* also youngsters who have set their heart on becoming cartoon animators or fashion designers and set out determinedly for a school that will help them to become one. It seems that hairdressers, cooks and dieticians are more likely to fall into this pattern. An interesting survey by Recruit Research (2,000 students in 44 senshu schools) found that more than 60 per cent of the students in hairdressing schools and cook/dietician schools said that they were doing what they intended all along to do. Only about 30 per cent made the same claim in the industrial, business and teacher-training schools. The percentages in the fashion, design, domestic science, art and music and nursing schools were in the 40s. The next question was only to those who had come to a senshu school as second best. What had been their first best? The industrial, design, art and music students were the disappointed college students — 60 per cent of the reluctant joiners, or 40 per cent of the whole. For hairdressers, cooks and dieticians who had hoped for something else, that something else was much more likely to have been an immediate job (Recruit 1985).

How far the second best is a best at all depends very much on the school. There is a general impression that it adds very little to the chances of career success. In the National Institute study, the 1,000 high school teachers in charge of their graduands' career guidance were asked to rate their agreement or disagreement with a number of judgements about the senshu schools. The statement with which there was the strongest general level of disagreement was: it is easier to get a job if you have been to a senshu school than if you have only been to a high school (p. 64). The question did not contain the proviso, but probably should have done, 'if you are looking for a job outside your home district'. A senshu-gakko qualification is a good deal less powerful than recommendation from a known local school.

But the extent to which this common judgement about the general run of senshu schools applies to particular schools is limited. The statement the high school teachers disagreed with least was: there is a great variation in the reliability of these schools. Undoubtedly, many of these schools are of poor quality. There are some, on the other hand, which have a high reputation for brisk efficiency, whose graduates are keenly sought by employers, and whose entrance examinations reject a good number of applicants. (More than 20 per cent of the industrial senshu school students in the Recruit Research survey reference had not got into their first-choice senshu school, nearly the same proportion of the cooks and dieticians, and close to 30 per cent of the nurses.)

Overall characterisations of the labour market's reception of senshu school graduates need, therefore, careful qualification, but the figures of an annual Recruit Research survey may nevertheless be worth quoting. (1,100 firms responded in 1985 out of a polled total of 5,200.) The proportion of firms which had recruited someone from a senshu school during the year has increased from 42 per cent in 1980 to 48–49 per cent in 1982–4. The industries which favoured them more than average were commerce and services, and also electrical, electronic and precision-machinery makers. The most common occupational specialties of those hired was data-processing (39 per cent of firms), followed by accountancy, book-keeping (38 per cent), secretarial (24 per cent), and foreign language skills (15 per cent). Those hired were more likely in 1984 than in 1981 to be treated for salary purposes as the equivalent of a two-year college graduate, though still 13 per cent of them were counted as high school graduates. (One firm of printed circuit board makers which was perfectly happy with raw high school graduates and saw no reason to explore the senshu graduate market gave as its reason the difficulty of fitting them into the salary system. Treat them as high school graduates and they are unhappy; treat them as college graduates and you make everybody else unhappy.)

One other change is that the senshu graduates are slightly more likely than they once were to be hired specifically for their

71

specialty — like the women hired from foreign-language schools by Mitsukoshi and sent on two-year contracts to their branch shops in France and Germany. (The standard journalistic cliche about senshu schools is that they produce 'combat-ready' employees — an interesting indication of the general expectation that normally employers have to do a lot of initial training before newly-hired employees are useful.) Still, however, about 50 per cent were taken on as general employees and not put specifically to work in the areas for which they were trained — and this applied, it appears, rather more to those who had received some specific qualification from that training than those who had not.

There is no easy way of assessing in any quantitative terms the contribution these schools make overall to the build-up of Japan's stock of human capital beyond the rather obvious propositions that:

Some senshu schools specializing in very specific occupational preparation — the hairdressing, cookery, surveying, nursing schools, for example — do a straightforward and on the whole craftsmanlike job of teaching a well-routinized and only slowly changing curriculum. The existence of a national qualifying examination in all these fields is an effective monitoring device to ensure that adequate standards are reached.

— Some which teach more general occupational skills, also of a relatively unchanging kind — English, accountancy — are also competent and of good reputation. A lot have been in the business for years, and have established good reputations. Many, once private proprietorships run for profit (as the bulk of senshu schools still are), have been turned into trusts of one kind or another on the original owner's death. It is perhaps proof of the ability of some of these schools to impart substantive skills rather than a mere graduating qualification, that some university students — the 'double-schoolers' — are said to be taking parallel courses at senshu schools in accountancy or computing.

— Some schools, which operate in the more fluid fields of business and computer studies and industrial technology, also perform a valuable service and are often well ahead of both vocational high schools and university engineering departments in teaching today's rather than yesterday's industrial and office techniques and practice. They are often expensive (£4–5,000 p.a. for industrial schools), but are well-equipped and use lively part-time teachers from good progressive firms, rather than dead-beat retirees who have been eased out of seats-by-the-window in firms in which they had long ceased to play an active part. Some, like the best software writers' schools, are major centres for the diffusion of important new industrial skills. Some can claim in their advertising that they had twenty times as many job offers (or, rather, invitations to apply) from firms as they had graduating students. The best ones have developed a regular relationship with major firms. Nihon Victor, for example, is reported to have nearly 1,000 senshu graduates on its books, nearly all drawn from one of seven or eight schools (*Nikkei Ryutsu*, 20 May 1985).

— But others, also, are exploitative and barely short of fraudulent in their pursuit of profit, relying on recruiting none-too-choosy 'might as well' students (and often over-recruiting beyond the declared capacity on which they fulfilled the space requirements for senshu registration purposes) giving fewer hours of instruction than they promised, and being none too concerned about either the professional competence or the pedagogical skills of those they hire to teach. Such schools are a good deal more common in the rapidly changing fields with more advertisable glamour. Should one, for instance, take seriously the school in Saitama which has newly established a 'Techno-lady Department' with courses in computers, the basic theory of office automation, practical secretarial work, English conversation and 'event production'? Perhaps some firms will.

The atmosphere of live-and-let-live hugger-mugger which pervades Japanese society (equally describable as the Japanese capacity for reaching reasonable and equitable solutions to problems without open confrontations) militates against the emergence of a genuinely independent consumers' association-type attempt to provide an assessment guide to such schools. The rough justice of such efforts would cause too many problems, and in Japan it is normally to the state rather than to citizen initiative that one looks for such services. The state has, indeed, used one implicit quality-vetting mechanism until recently. The Ministry of Labour legally retains control of all job placement services. It is illegal to operate a personnel agency without authorization, and all the placement services of universities are so recognized. This authorization was until recently granted only to about 200 of the larger and better-established schools — which were able to advertise the fact in their brochures and make claims about their *bairitsu* — the ratio of employers' requests to numbers of graduating students. The other 3,000 schools — at least the conscientious ones among them — were not, of course, deterred from trying to provide the same service for their students, and there was never any question of prosecution. The Ministry has now bowed to reality and made all senshu schools automatically authorized for personnel placement work.

One other form of official intervention: 123 schools are recognized by the Ministry of Education as bringing middle-school graduates up to the level of high school graduation, hence eligible for university entrance. But this is a minor function of the senshu schools, affecting, it is estimated, only 80,000 of the million-plus students. The schools are now overwhelmingly concerned with the further training of high-school leavers.

PUBLIC ASSISTANCE

This is not to say that government agencies are not concerned with the senshu-gakko and are content to leave them entirely to the market. There are always officials ready to offer a little administrative guidance. One school which was starting a new course to train biotechnology lab technicians told reporters that they had at first intended tentatively to introduce biotechnology as a minor part of the pharmacy course until they were urged by an official to make it a full-scale department in view of its importance for the future.

In financial terms, however, apart from the small number of state, prefectural and municipal schools among them, the senshu-gakko constitute an almost pure market sector. Assistance for students from the State Scholarship Fund is on an exiguous scale. The maximum grant for high-school leavers attending a private institution and living away from home is £170 a month and there is a quota of 2,400 students a year (plus a quota of 1,200 students attending public senshu schools — the nurses, etc. — who get a lesser amount). Middle-school leavers on high-school-equivalent courses — 600 of them — get half that amount.

Total state subsidization was reckoned (*Nikkei*, 5 June 1985) to amount in 1985 only to ¥1.7bn or about £7.5m — mostly in the form of the above-mentioned loans to students, overseas aid funds for foreign students, and a small sum from the national fund for large-scale instructional equipment In addition there were reduced-interest loans of ¥2.4bn (£10.8m) from the Private Educational Institutions Fund for school buildings.

This sum, however, probably includes only monies disbursed under the auspices of the Ministry of Education. There is also a certain amount of assistance available to nursing schools from the Ministry of Health, and the Ministry of Labour and its prefectural Labour Department counterparts provide some assistance to certain senshu schools.

For example, a hairdressing school in Fukushima, with 88 pupils on a one-year course in 1986 had a dual legal personality. On the one hand it was a legal trust (*shadan hojin*), an association of 441 local barbers who had each made a capital contribution of about £90 and paid an annual subscription of £5. About a tenth of the annual expenditure of some ¥30m came from donations (including ¥100,000 from a textbook supplier) and about two-thirds from student fees. At the same time it was also constituted as a Vocational Training School, performing delegated training under the terms of the Vocational Training Act. In this capacity it had another budget amounting to ¥11m and in that capacity alone was entitled to receive a subsidy for 55 student places from the prefecture. The whole point of this fictional division of the budget was to receive a subsidy of ¥2½m, the total effect of which was to reduce the fees to be paid by all its 88 students by about 8 per cent, from £1,750 to £1,620.

Even if all these additional sources of support are taken into account, however, the total public subsidy is marginal. Total annual fee payments by students at senshu schools probably amount to around ¥660bn or about £3bn.

6

Training in the enterprise

Except when they get foreign visitors coming to ask about them, Japanese firms do not make a big thing of their training programmes. They rather take them for granted. The reasons why they do so have a lot to do with the 'community' character of Japanese enterprises. Those community characteristics are found both in large and in small firms, but it is in the large firms that they are more clearly expressed in formal institutionalized rules.

There are about 93 million Japanese aged 15 and over. Sixty per cent of them are gainfully employed. Nearly a quarter of those are self-employed or family workers. Another 17–18 per cent of them are part-time or temporary workers. That leaves about 36 million who are regular full-time workers. Of these less than a fifth — 6.5 million — are in private enterprises which employ over a thousand workers. The public sector with similar conditions of service, accounts for another 4 million.

So the 10 million-plus in the large-firm and public sector are by no means a majority of the Japanese work-force. Nevertheless, it is among them that most of the difficult learning goes on, and in the large-firm sector that the workers of the higher school-diagnosed learning ability are concentrated. It is not surprising, therefore, that most of the available information about enterprise training concerns the larger enterprises, and it is with those that we begin.

LIFETIME EMPLOYMENT AND TRAINING

The presumption of lifetime employment, at least for a firm's core labour force, still provides a strong justification for firms to invest in the training of their workers. Over the labour market as a whole, something like 40 per cent of new recruits leave within three years of entering their first job, but this proportion is a good deal smaller among the employees of large firms, smaller for high school than for middle school graduates, and very much smaller yet for university graduates.

And it should not be forgotten that, nowadays, a substantial proportion of the new entrants to the labour force are graduates. As Table 2.1 shows, over a third of new recruits in finance, banking, insurance and real estate in 1985 were university graduates. In manufacturing almost a quarter. Add in the (mostly female) two-year college graduates and the totals are 63 per cent and 33 per cent respectively. If one takes the figures for male recruits into manufacturing alone, 37 per cent came from a university, including 23 per cent — almost six out of every ten — from a science department, among them 4 per cent with Master's degrees.

The long-term perspective induced by the lifetime employment assumption has a number of consequences.

Recruitment is for a career, not for a job. Selection criteria concentrate, consequently (leaving aside, for the moment, the very important personality factors) on demonstrated ability to learn rather than on particular job competences already acquired.

Employers are, consequently, more likely than employers in countries with greater job mobility, to be content, even when recruiting science, engineering, economics and business studies graduates, if they have a good general grounding in their subject as a solid basis for on-the-job training. The complaint that universities do not provide the sort of practical vocational training that makes graduates immediately useful in specific jobs is not often heard. Nevertheless, that general grounding is seen to be of considerable importance for science and engineering graduates — and also, though to a rather lesser degree, for economics and business studies graduates. A bright lawyer or political scientist would be expected to be as useful as an economics graduate in a corporate finance department within a matter of months rather than years, but not so a mechanical engineer switched to bio-technology.

Views about the depth of the grounding required have changed over the last twenty years. Previously, few companies had anything in their salary and promotion structures to encourage those with a BA degree — and, in effect, as described in Chapter 3, only two years of specialist science and engineering training — to stay for a two-year Master's course. There was no clear likelihood that, either at 25 or at 30, the MA would be ahead of the BA in either salary or responsibility. The advantage of getting recruits earlier at the BA stage, and starting them earlier on all the specific learning they had to do, was seen to outweigh the deepening and broadening of theoretical understanding which a Master's course would offer. Some firms still hold the same view, but preference, and career advantage, is now increasingly given to holders of Master's degrees — almost universally for those entering the R & D departments of large firms, less universally for those entering production departments.

A third consequence of the lifetime employment assumption — and of the mixture of seniority and performance-merit which guides the personnel placement system — is that frequent retraining is seen as a necessary part of a normal career. In most firms the managerial and technologist functions are structured into a series of ranks — vice-section chief, section chief, vice-departmental chief, etc. Promotions, a rank at a time, frequently involve a change of department and function, and the need for a substantial new learning process. Those who are identified at an early stage as high-flyers probably destined for senior management positions, are deliberately rotated through key departments in order to maximize the breadth of their knowledge of the firm's business. Specialization is more common from the mid-30s onwards, but still is often not definitive.

A further implication of lifetime employment: diversification of the firm's business often by hiving off divisions into subsidiaries becomes an essential way of coping with the contraction of established markets — a prospect faced with increasing frequency by large corporations since the mid-1970s, with the change in energy costs and new materials affecting the competitiveness of basic industries, changes in trade patterns and changes in technology affecting almost everybody. Since a major purpose of diversification is to avoid redundancies (and the serious damage to morale of the breach of the lifetime employment guarantee which redundancies involve) diversification through acquisition is rarely the preferred form. (A contested takeover is in any case taboo in Japan, and negotiated mergers take a lot of negotiating.) The corporation moves into new areas by adapting and diverting its existing resources, creating internal project teams — shipbuilding companies moving into plant engineering, steel companies into plastics and ceramic materials, textile companies into cosmetics and biotechnology. Increasingly, in recent years, companies have sought to accelerate the process of building up new expertise by mid-career recruitment — bringing in people with specific skills. A twice-monthly journal, *Beruf*, was started in 1982, specifically to provide a channel for technologist and technician job advertisements.

The October 1985 issue, for example, had advertisements for people with experience in opt-electronics, software and lasers from the leading sewing machine and electronic printer maker, Juki, for semi-conductor circuit designers from Nissan, for silicon wafer experts from a new subsidiary of Japan Steel.

Such new recruits provide a core of knowledge and experience of the technology into which firms seek to diversify, and this recent loosening up of the technologist job market represents a change from traditional practice. But still the bulk of the staff developing new projects in diversifying firms are drawn from the firms' core lifetime-employed staff, and they face new learning tasks often of considerable magnitude.

A further implication of all the structured need for continuing new learning implicit in the personnel system: if everybody expects frequently to be a learner, so everybody expects frequently to have to be a teacher. Newcomers to a department are not expected to have immediate competence in their job. Those who are competent expect to have to help them to learn.

OTHER ASSUMPTIONS RELEVANT TO TRAINING

There are two other assumptions fundamental to the training programmes of Japanese firms. The first is related to, but not a necessary consequence of the lifetime-employment assumption. It is what one might call the 'participation assumption' — the assumption that employees, having a strong (lifetime) stake in the firm and its success, also are emotionally identified with it and so can be motivated to make extra effort as may be necessary to improve their existing skills and acquire new ones, not only by the prospect that they will gain personal advantage. That must certainly be a consideration; a higher performance rating by their pleased superiors carries the possibility of a better bonus or faster promotion or a more interesting job. But one should not underestimate, also, a concern to be able better to contribute to the firm's success. People do not have to have the prospect of a better job or a salary supplement in order to be persuaded to take a course. Willingness to learn is part of what one is hired for, not just the ability to perform a particular type of job. As one would expect, this sort of motivation has more reality the higher the individual's pay and responsibility. It works more for the university-educated manager than for a shopfloor worker — as in any country. But it is the managers who have more learning to do.

The other assumption is that employees' learning can be not only to a high degree self-motivated, but also quite self-reliant. Japan's very thorough basic education system produces a very high general level of literacy and of written as well as oral articulateness. It produces people capable of following carefully detailed and complex written instructions — as anyone who has bought a Japanese computer printer might infer from the manual which accompanies it. This means that a lot of learning is based on informal production of job specifications and procedure manuals meticulously written out by supervisors and used as teaching material for self-teaching by newcomers to a job. You do not just stand by Nelly; you read what Nelly has thoughtfully and meticulously written about what she knows.

TRAINING BUDGETS

All this helps to explain why Japanese firms' training budgets seem rarely impressive. Table 6.1 gives the figures from a recent (1984) Ministry of Labour survey of labour costs in 6,000 firms with 30 or more employees (Chingin 1984; let us call it Sample 1). Average cash remuneration in these firms (wages and bonuses) amounted to nearly 300,000 yen per month. Total non-wage costs came to 53,000 yen per employee, of which 1,022 yen — about £5 a month at current exchange rates — was spent on education and training — less than was spent on sports and entertainment, and about 0.3 per cent of cash remuneration. The figure ranged from 0.5 per cent in the largest firms with more than 5,000 employees to 0.1 per cent in firms with fewer than 100. In terms of turnover, the range is 0.1 per cent to 0.02 per cent, with an average around 0.07 per cent — rather less than the 0.15 per cent which a 1985 MSC-commissioned survey (IFF 1985) estimated to be typical — deplorably typical — for British firms.

The annual nature of this survey gives some idea of year-to-year fluctuations for the last fifteen years. Overall, it suggests, training budgets have been growing a little faster than wages or employers' contributions to social security (11.8 per cent per annum, 1973–83, compared with 10.4 and 7.6 per cent respectively; RH 1985). The biggest increase — of 20 per cent over the previous year — came in 1975; the year of zero growth; in many sectors of an actual fall in output. Japanese firms do not respond to recession by cutting training budgets, but by putting surplus man-hours to improving skill levels.

Table 6.1 Expenditure on education and training by size of firm **(Manufacturing only)**

(Labour cost survey 1984)

Size of Enterprise (No. of Employees)	Non-wage costs as a percentage of wage costs		
	Total	Sport & Entertainment	Education & Training
> 5,000	21.0	0.5	0.5
1,000-4,999	19.1	0.4	0.5
300-999	16.6	0.3	0.3
100-299	15.6	0.4	0.2
30-99	15.1	0.4	0.1
All sizes	18.2	0.4	0.3

Source: Rodosho, Seisaku-chosa-bu, (Ministry of Labour, Policy Research Bureau). *Chingin, rodo-jikan seido to sogo-chosa hokoku* (Survey of wages, hours, and conditions of service), 1984

Another survey conducted by a training magazine — a postal survey which elicited replies from forty-nine firms — gives rather more detail about the nature of these budgets (Sample 2: Kigyo 1986). It makes clear, first of all, that 'the training budget' is a very loose concept indeed in Japanese firms. It often does not include:

— Any cost estimates for time spent in informal on-the-job learning.
— Salaries of the administrative staff of the training department, and frequently, even, of the instructors at the firm's training school.
— Capital costs or maintenance costs of training schools.
— Similar costs at the multi-purpose buildings which are maintained by many firms partly as a recreation centre, as a meeting place for Quality Circle teams, or for various special interest clubs, as a hotel for visiting staff from branch offices, and also — usually, primarily — as a training centre for ad hoc courses.
— Travel costs for staff attending courses (which come out of a separate travel budget).

Matsushita Electric, for instance, which has a training budget of 0.1 per cent of turnover (it still amounts to some ¥3bn or about £4.5m) estimates that this figure should be multiplied perhaps four or five times if indirect costs were to be included (NK, 1986, p. 135).

What, then, do these training budgets cover, and what is the relative priority given to various types of training?

The largest single item (23 per cent of total expenditure) is for meeting places, hotels, etc. for the firm's own courses — an item on which those with their own establishments make considerable savings. Closely following it, at 21 per cent, is the cost of sending members of the firm to courses run by other organizations.

The cost effectiveness of this expenditure is probably higher than in Britain for two reasons. First, accommodation is not lavish, to judge from the advertisements in the training magazines. A hotel not far from the centre of Tokyo offers meeting rooms, overnight stay and three meals for ¥11,200 — only about £50 even at an exchange rate which prices a cup of coffee between £1.10 and £1.80. Secondly, on the effectiveness side, Japanese are great note-takers — and when the course is of wider interest many of the participants will be expected to use those notes to give talks themselves when they get back to their own firms or departments. This is especially the case for outside courses intended to bring people up to date on the latest trends in markets, fashions, technologies, or legal requirements.

Travel and per diems for attendance at such courses (sometimes, but obviously not always, charged to a general travel account rather than to the training account), made up 12 per cent, and the purchase of teaching materials, texts, subscriptions to correspondence courses, etc. made up 8 per cent. This leaves 36 per cent in the 'miscellaneous other' expenditures, ranging from fees for visiting lecturers to stationery for the training department.

One or two of the respondents gave details of the cost of particular items: for example, a four months' induction training for 135 university graduates was costed at ¥4.5m (£20,000), a two month induction course for 380 graduates at ¥2.8m (£12,000).

OFF-THE-JOB LECTURE COURSES (ZAGAKU OR 'SIT STUDY')

External courses, as might be expected, are much more expensive than internal ones. For the 21 per cent of their budgets which the 23 manufacturing firms spent on them, the sample recorded only 35 course attendances involving 147 people (43 of them on a single course) — to which should be added five people sent abroad and 20 sent to the Tsukuba Science Exhibition. By contrast, over 9,000 people were involved in internal courses in those firms. The courses are such as may be found almost anywhere — corporate strategy for top management, marketing seminars, a course for newly appointed directors, orientation courses for middle-managers, a basic accountancy course, a course for shopfloor supervisors, Keio Business School's management development programme. Perhaps less common elsewhere are what appear to be uplift courses — e.g., a PHP leader seminar, PHP being the Peace, Happiness and Prosperity philosophy of the veteran business leader Matsushita. The advertisements suggest that the incidence of high-flown, high pressure charlatanry is not necessarily lower in the Japanese training industry than elsewhere. One seminar which could well find a place in Berg's *Great Training Robbery* is called (in English) 'Creative My Life' and seems to be for managers who show signs of mid-life crisis trouble. The advertisement tells us that:

> The seminar is for 40-year olds who want to take life head-on, who want to lead a creative, active, vigorous work life. For those of us who have opted for being company men, to live a splendid life is to live a splendid company life. What we need to do is to capitalize to the full on our accumulated experience in the company and look forward to the future with burning enthusiasm for the present.

A recent survey which covered 325 firms gives a certain amount of detail about coverage and attitudes towards, and beliefs about, training (Sample 3: NK, 1985). Though be it noted that this sample is probably biased towards firms which are enthusiastic about training, since they are the 16 per cent who did, not the 84 per cent who did not, provide replies to a postal questionnaire sent to 2,010 firms.

On the direction of training effort, figures are provided on the proportion of firms which reckon to have spent, in 1983, more than ¥30,000 (£135) per head, on the training of different categories of workers. Thirty-seven per cent claim to have done so for managers; 31 per cent for sales and administrative staff; 23 per cent for R & D staff; 18 per cent for other technical staff; 11 per cent for shopfloor workers. Respondents who estimated that more than 50 per cent of their managers had been on some kind of off-the-job training during the year made up 33 per cent of the sample; 16 per cent of the sample claimed to have trained more than 50 per cent of their sales and administrative staff, and 9 per cent of the sample more than 50 per cent of shopfloor workers.

Initial induction training is still the largest item in most firms' budget. Many of the larger firms have substantial training schools for craftsmen/technicians. An example is the NEC school which recruits seventy-five carefully selected high-school graduates (no

Table 6.2 Curriculum of the NEC two-year training school for multi-skill technicians

Hours	First Year	Second Year	Hours
240	Classroom Work (Sit-Study) Academic		140
80	Maths: Basic calculation, plane geometry & mechanical drawing, trigonometry, linear algebra	Infinitesimal differential calculus, Boolean algebra	35
40	English: written & spoken	English written & spoken	35
80	Sports: physical training	Sports	70
40	General: Writing technical reports		
575	Specialist		590
70	Basics of Electrical Engineering. AC/DC. Magnetism & static electricity, resistance, circuits.		
45	Ditto II: Diodes, Transistors, Bias Circuits amplification circuits	Ditto III: Transmitter circuits, FM circuits, AM circuits	45
		Production Engineering: Production planning, standard times, quality control, cost accounting, production methods	80
45	Control Engineering I: Feedback control, basic circuits, sequential circuits	Control Engineering II: Control devices, sensors, transducers	60
		Mechanical Devices Transmission & transformation of forces: gears, cams, differentials	60
45	Metal Machining, I; Tools & Materials, cutting techniques	Ditto II: Founding, welding, moulding, forging, surface treatment	60
45	Measurement: Length, surfaces, angles, accuracy & error measurement, vibration, temperature	Measurement: Transformation & flows, tests for transmission characteristics, pulsing characteristics	60

Hours	First Year	Second Year	Hours
45	Health & Safety I: Three basic principles: standard working practices	Safety II Health inspection, first aid, legal requirement, work environment	45
60	Materials Ferrous, non-ferrous metals, non-metallic materials, heat treatment, materials tests	Mechanics Moments, escapements	70
60	Materials Mechanics: Stress & torque, stretch & compression, metal fatigue	Electrical Circuits Semi-conductors, equalization circuits, static characteristics & amplification of transistors, sequential circuits, MSI circuits	70
60	Design & Draughtsmanship: Tools & materials: uses & types of lines, basic techniques, JIS standards		
60	Elements of Machinery: Sealing devices, axles & bearings, transmission devices		
40	Microcomputing I: Transmission instructions, processing instructions, inputting programs	Micro-computing II CPVO, interfacing, programming methods	40
	Practical Work *1. Basic Skills*		
70	Measurement & fine shaving adjustment, basic techniques & tools	Ditto	10
235	Basic hand operations Filing, finishing, heat treatment	Ditto	60
270	Basic machine techniques Use of lathes, milling machine, boring machines, planers etc. conventional	Ditto Plus CNC lathes & machining centres	185
995			620

Hours	First Year	Second Year	Hours
			442
40	Basic fitting technqiues tool assembly	Ditto	40
30	Tool sharpening For all types of cutting & drilling	Ditto	10
80	Health & Safety Safety in finishing, machining & electrical work	Ditto	50
120	Basic electrical techniques: soldering, insulating & wrapping, wiring	Basic electrical measurement	30
30	Circuit diagrams How to write & read	Oscilloscope	115
40	Circuit construction	Circuit design & assembly	120
80	Experiments in Electrical Engineering: circuit design, relay sequence controls	Making basic electronic instruments	
150	2. Applied Work		
110	Jig and tool assembly	Assembly, testing, repair of machines	402
40	Making basic electronic devices	Repair of analogue circuits	20
		Testing & measurement of electronic instruments	20

Summary: Distribution of Hours

	First Year	Second year
Classroom		
Academic	240	140
Vocational	575	590
Practical		
Basic Mechanical	645	305
Basic Electrical	270	265
Health & Safety	80	50
Applied	150	442
Total	1,960	1,792

particular preference for graduates of technical high-schools) for an intensive two-year course, the curriculum for which is detailed in Table 6.2. The school started as a one-year course for 15-year-olds in 1939, switched to high-school graduate recruitment in 1960 and was extended to two years in 1970. In 1986 it was officially recognized by the Ministry of Education as a two-year junior college.

This course is intended to train an elite of highly skilled technicians — 'people who can perform roles intermediate between craftsmen and technologists; craftsmen who can talk the same language as technologists'. They are expected to be the foremen of the next decade. It remains an unusual firm which has such an elaborated training system. Of the 325 firms in Sample 3 (the more training-minded of the 2,000 biggest firms, it will be recalled) 44 per cent said they had some sort of training school or training centre and 27 per cent said they had one which contributed to the training of shopfloor workers, though this most certainly does not mean that anything like that percentage had craft-technician training schemes of the NEC type in-house.

And even in NEC, of course, the schools absorb only a minority of the annual intake. Initial training for most new employees is a rather shorter affair, which may involve some learning of basic skills in common use in the firm, but also includes a good deal of general instruction in the nature of the firm's business, as well as a good deal of morale building, loyalty building and general spiritual integration (see Rohlen 1974 for a splendidly detailed description of the graduate induction programme of a West Japan bank). The length of the induction training varies. In the forty-nine firms in Sample 2, the range was from one week to two months for high-school graduates and from one to five months for university graduates. Rarely is there more than a week of classroom instruction for a new high-school worker intake, but many firms do rotate new recruits around the firm — a week at a time in each department over a four month period in one 500-employee factory. For graduates the period of rotation through short-term assignments for learning purposes may last as long as two years. How much this counts as a formal training programme accounts for the wide variation in reports of the length of initial training.

Much of this training is opportunistic rather than planned. When a junior is in an explicitly trainee status, his seniors take every opportunity that offers to pass on their skills. When one of the authors once landed in the northern port of Hakodate and had his passport duly stamped on board the boat, he was puzzled to be asked to call in the Immigration Office when he went ashore. There he was fussed over, settled in a soft chair and given a cup of tea while the Immigration officer took his assistant through the mysteries of a British passport — a relatively rare commodity in those parts. An American training in a Japanese firm thought he was being singled out for special treatment when he was taken on what was evidently a learning visit when one of his older colleagues had business in the Japanese patent office. He found that this was actually scheduled as something to be fitted in when opportunity occurred in the course of every Japanese engineer's training (Bhasavanich 1985).

Mid-career training of a formal kind is found in a minority of firms. NEC, for instance, has the following formal off-the-job training courses, primarily for craft and technical workers, used partly for upgrading initial basic training, partly in re-training for job changes.

Electronics 1	96 hours
Electronics 2	96 hours
Use of the syncho-scope	24 hours
Feedback controls 1	96 hours
Feedback controls 2	96 hours
Personal computers 1	48 hours
Personal computers 2	56 hours
Basic programming	40 hours
Numerical control	48 hours
CNC machining centres	64 hours
Mechanical drawing	64 hours
Jig & equipment maintenance	120 hours

A more common form of regular institutionalized training is the pre-promotion course for middle-managers or for shopfloor supervisors, staff college courses for those about to be appointed to senior management positions. One electronics firm with 17,000 employees, for example, has a nine-month course for shopfloor supervisors and six-month courses for senior managers. In Fujitsu, a selection/training course for early-30s section chiefs consists of taking a number of correspondence courses and writing a thesis on some aspect of the firm's organization, under the supervision of a senior manager (McCormick 1986).

NON-FORMAL IN-FIRM TRAINING

Accounts of Japanese in-firm training usually give great emphasis to

these formally institutionalized off-the-job training programmes —
and it is true that in some large firms they are impressive in extent.
But to dwell too long on them would be to reinforce the assumptions
commonly made by representatives of the training industries of Japan's
competitors — namely that the way to meet the Japanese challenge
is by bigger and better organized formal courses — of the kind which
they are specialists in providing.

What the Japanese example draws attention to, rather, is the
importance of less formal alternatives — mutual teaching in the
workplace, and self-study paid for either by the firm or the individual
— both one-way learning through books and cassettes, and interactive
learning, either through correspondence courses, or, rarely, electronic
learning programmes.

A question in the Sample 3 study asked about the methods used
to train manual workers and foremen. The table below shows the
percentage of firms saying that they made some use of a particular
method.

It will be seen that, for shopfloor workers especially, and even
for shop supervisors, the lower half of the table greatly exceeds the
upper half in importance. They are the activities which justify calling
the typical Japanese firm a learning environment. A few words by
way of commentary on particular items.

| Method | % of firms using the method for: | |
	Shopfloor workers	Foremen
External training agency, public sector	4	12
External training agency, private sector	4	22
Firm's own training school	27	44
Older, more experienced colleagues	58	21
Training by engineering & managerial staff	26	24
Rotation around jobs	19	19
Correspondence education	17	20
Small group participation, Quality Circles	60	20

Older, more experienced workers

We have already discussed the importance of on-the-job training as
part of what are formally defined as initial training programmes —
the way casual opportunities are used as grist to the training mill.
The point to be made here is that training periods do not formally
end; they only fade away. All juniors are potential pupils.

And a lot of this teaching and learning is systematic. Recall what was said earlier about both the 'participation assumption' and the 'literacy and articulacy assumption'. Supervisors often write down for the benefit of their juniors what they see as the important and non-obvious know-how they have got from doing their job. Juniors do not just stand by Nelly; they read what Nelly has been persuaded to put on formal record. Add to this the assumption of seniority-constrained promotion. Promotion on the shopfloor is only seniority-constrained, not seniority-determined. Able juniors can be pushed ahead of their seniors, but the age gap which they can overleap is limited — perhaps three to four years at the younger ages, ten to fifteen years at higher ages. Moreover, promotion frequently involves a lateral shift of department. Hence few people with responsibility for teaching their juniors have any reason to fear that if those juniors mastered their job they might displace them. Add also the general cultural assumptions about the duty of benevolence required of superiors in hierarchical relations — a benevolence which is rewarded with respect and deference (an older Suzuki may call his junior 'Tanaka' but get 'Mr. Suzuki' in return). All of these add up to the general expectation that teaching is part of the supervisor's job. How well he brings on his juniors is one of the criteria by which a senior worker will be rated; one of the things which will determine his chances of promotion, in some firms the size of his bonus.

Training by technical and managerial staff

This occurs with much greater frequency in Japanese than in most European or American factories, and is frequently mentioned by Japanese who have been abroad, and by British observers of Japanese firms operating in Britain (White and Trevor 1983). The importance for this Japanese characteristic increases as the pace of technical change accelerates. When a new product is being produced, or a production system rearranged, a taken-for-granted part of the production engineering involved is for the engineers and work study experts to hold formal sessions to explain the changes, and to instruct — as hands-on as is necessary — those who have to do something new just how that new thing is to be done. Lorriman (1986) estimates that Japanese companies employ twice as many development engineers as British companies, and one can see why.

This process is extended beyond the firm. Mitsubishi Electric's Kyoto factory, which produces 100 model variations in its TV sets and VTRs per annum, never has fewer than two or three engineers out spending a few days with a sub-contractor making sure his workers know how to get a new sub-assembly right.

One pump manufacturer with 500 employees has recently taken steps to put internal mutual instruction on a more formal basis. It has for some time required, as most firms with a formal training budget require, annual submission of training plans from each department — what sort of lectures they want laid on for whom; whom they want to put on what external or correspondence courses, etc. In 1985 departmental managers were required to answer two further questions: what do members of your department need to know or better understand about the work of other departments in order to do their work better? And: what do you wish other departments better understood about your operations in order to make your work more efficient? A technical committee was convened to review the proposals for possible action, and the first page of its report is translated in Table 6.3. It will be seen that the programme drawn up involved a good deal of cross-departmental lecturing — designers explaining the principles of their designs to assemblers; testers explaining the testing criteria to the electricians who have to design the equipment, etc.

Job rotation

For the training of graduates and of potential high-flyer technicians and foremen, deliberate rotation around the firm is a standard part of the learning-teaching process. It happens at two levels: induction rotation — the process already described of having new recruits spend their first six months, say, working in various departments a week or two at a time — and more long-term rotation, when people are given regular eighteen month/two-year postings, but the posts are chosen so as to make up optimal packages of useful experience — with the greater care, the greater the promise shown of being of potential senior management calibre. For shopfloor workers, the prime form of rotation is within a single department. One major purpose is to achieve flexible worker deployment; when everyone can do two or three jobs absences are easier to cover. But other advantages are also consciously sought — better co-operation can be achieved when everybody understands everybody else's job; permanent changes of job can happen more quickly if slack periods have been used for learning in advance; the symbolic recognition of self-development as an end in itself helps to preserve a desirable 'learning society'

91

Table 6.3 Dengyosha Pump Company: proposals for interdepartmental mutual teaching programme

Need for				
Which Dept.?	Overseas Plant Installation	Plant designers	Machinery Dept. or Technical Dept.	Running Test Dept.
To teach Whom?	Plant Designers	Running Test. Dept.	Turbo-pump design department	Electrical Dept.
What?	Problems cropping up in plant installation	Problems cropping up in test-proving of installed systems	The limits of the company's metal-cutting capacity	Means of measurement of capacity/efficiency of pumps/fans
Why?	To standardize design procedures & raise design quality	Better planning of on-spot tests through knowledge of complete plant system	To avoid designing the impossible	So that they better understand the product aimed for
When?	May-Sept. 86	May-Sept. 86	a.s.a.p	c. Aug. 86
Action	No formal arrangement Design and Installation sections to consult on problems as they arise	Ditto	Ueda from Machinery Dept. to give lectures Aug. 86 to one person from each of the turbine design groups	Rep. from RTD — lectures July/Aug.

Need for

Which Dept?	Electrical Department	Electrical Department	Headquarters Technical Staff	Factory Technical Staff
To teach Whom?	Welders in No. 4 Dept.	Crane operators in Depts. 1-4	Factory Technical Staff	Design supervisors — especially in pump section
What?	Basics of Electricity	Maintenance & inspection of cranes	Recent trends in customer specification of materials required	Optimal use of special steels
Why?	To prevent electrocution accidents	Accident prevention. (They already perform basic maintenance. Need to go further)	To get better standardization of which range of materials for which purposes	We use a lot of special steels, but a bit haphazardly
When?	Aug. 86?	Summer 86	July 86	June 86
Action	Mr. Nabeya from Electrical Dept. at his convenience, lectures	Mr. Mizuguchi from Electrical Dept. Talks & practical instruction	Not to be proceeded with	Mr. Fukazawa or Yamamoto, plus outside lecturer, for up to 15 designers, July

atmosphere, and the sense of achievement when a new skill is mastered adds to work motivation. Bhasanavich reports an engineer as justifying the decision to buy a new foreign machine the pay-off from which was not entirely certain on the grounds that the workers would enjoy learning to use it (Bhasanavich 1986).

Small group work: Quality Circles

As is by now well known, Quality Circles are not just about product quality, but more generally about taking thought in small groups as to how the efficiency of the group's work operations might, by whatever means, be improved. This often involves a good deal of useful learning. To start with, there is a standard set of analytical techniques which the group study — simple operational research methods of defect analysis: tree diagrams, Pareto cumulations, etc. Secondly, when the group has chosen its problem theme, it, or some of its delegated members, may set about learning something which has a bearing on the problems of solution. If they decide it would be a good idea to deepen the wastepit in a galvanizing plant so that it has to be pumped out less frequently, thereby reducing the number of heavily-energy-consuming start-ups of the pump, somebody will need to find out just how much more electricity the start-up involves; what the pit-lining has to be, given the corrosive character of the liquids; how much deepening the pit would cost. They might use QC funds to buy a book. More likely, they would use their right to call on the engineering staff to come and give them a lecture.

CORRESPONDENCE COURSES

A lot of the learning that goes in Japanese firms — as in the example just given — is learning by individuals who have been out to buy a book. The market for such literature is considerable and it is well supplied. One well-stocked bookshop, for example, had on its shelves no fewer than ninety-three different books with either 'QC' or 'TQC' (Total Quality Control) in the title. They were all slim, all quite cheap, all in brightly covered covers, and all directed at the worried shopfloor supervisor or small group leader who wants to know how to do his job properly. Nikka-giren, the industrial publisher, claims to have published 600,000 copies of its biggest QC seller.

The QC market must surely be the biggest market of all because the most general, but even for more esoteric skills the range of available textbooks is astonishing. (So also is the range of reference books and directories — from encyclopaedias of welding techniques to annual directories of think-tanks.)

But a large part of this self-study is through correspondence courses. A glance at the advertisements in almost any Japanese newspaper reveals the wide variety and range of correspondence courses. They fall into a number of categories. Some are for straight-forward replacement of formal education — university correspondence courses, high-school courses and the like. The Ministry of Education's new University of the Air has added considerably to the range and quality of offerings of this sort, but with increasing affluence and the general spread of education aspirations, the numbers seeking to take advantage of these second-chance routes to educational qualifications is much less than in the immediate post-war period when poverty truncated many schooling careers well before learning capacities or aspirations were exhausted. It is probably true to say that the contribution of these courses to Japan's industrial or business capacity or social efficiency, whatever it may have been in the past, is now marginal, if not negligible.

A second category is the large number of supplementation courses for those still in school or college — predominantly courses in English and calligraphy. (The main guide lists twenty-four of the latter, some specializing in ballpen calligraphy, a minority in traditional brush calligraphy of which one, at ¥45,000 (£200) uses video cassettes.)

A third category (into which the brush calligraphy courses ought perhaps also to be included) is the useful or enjoyable, possibly money-earning, arts. These are predominantly, but not exclusively, for the housewife market. Into this category come a wide variety of musical, dressmaking, DIY, gardening, advertising copywriting, poetry-writing, or foreign language courses — including also the three-month, ¥30,000 (£140) course in The Art of Translating English Romantic Fiction, offered by an enterprising publisher on the lookout for promising talent to help meet Japan's insatiable demand for the products of Mills and Boone.

This leaves the fourth and largest category which concerns us here, the specifically business and technical courses which are of considerable importance for in-firm training. Since the 1984 revision of the Vocational Training Act employers have been able to apply for a subsidy of one-quarter (one-third in the case of small and medium enterprises) of their own contributions towards the costs incurred by their employees in following such correspondence courses (as well as courses at outside training centres). The 1986 Ministry of Labour budget provides ¥783 million for this purpose (approximately £5.5m) — a 50 per cent increase over the previous year. The Ministry has recently published a comprehensive guide to the nearly 1,200 courses which are considered eligible for subsidy (Jiko-keihatsu 1986). Some details of these courses are to be found in Tables 6.4 and 6.5.

As might be expected the largest categories are for administrative, accounting and secretarial skills of the sort which lend themselves most easily to correspondence tuition. There is also, however, a large number of technical courses which primarily provide theoretical

Table 6.4 Correspondence courses recognized as eligible for Ministry of Labour support grants

General managerial	31
General: foremen	23
General: middle management (chūken)	19
Basic principles of OJT	7
Clerical, secretarial, personnel	31
Accounting, financial	47
Production control, stock management, etc.	7
Other clerical and administrative	21
Commercial, marketing and general services	103
Finance and real estate	65
Manufacturing research, development, design	45
Manufacturing processes, control & maintenance	68
Food industry	7
Printing industry	5
Steel industry	71
Manufacturing production engineering	55
Construction industry	9
Draughtsmanship, tracing	19
Agriculture and nutrition	11
Domestic appliance repair	8
Miscellaneous (statistics, maths, calligraphy, quality control, value engineering, investment analysis, etc.)	81
Personal computers	52
Micro computers	29
Other computing	11
English	85
Courses leading to state qualification: business	12
Courses leading to state qualification: technical	27
Miscellaneous and life-enhancing (Building memory power, persuasive power, intellectual vitality etc.)	70

Source: Jiko-keihatsu, 1986

Table 6.5 Provenance of correspondence courses recognized as eligible for Ministry of Labour support grants

Operating Agency	Operating Agencies	Computer Courses	No. of Other Technical Courses	Other Courses	Total Courses
Commercial Firms	51	44	140	367	551
Non-Profit Agencies					
Iron & Steel Technical College	1	0	69	0	69
College of Industrial Efficiency (Sangyō Nōritsu Daigaku)	1	16	29	103	148
Japan Institute of Vocational Training (Shokugyō Kunren Daigakkō)	1	0	26	0	26
Other Universities, Colleges, Schools	15	1	5	68	74
Professional & Industrial Associations	31	23	67	180	270
Japan Centre for Vocational Education (Nihon Ginō Kyōiku Kaihatsu Sentaa)	1	9	38	8	55
Consumer Cooperatives Association	1	0	0	6	6
Small or Medium Enterprise Agency	1	1	2	1	4
Total	103	94	376	733	1,203

Source: Jiko-keihatsu, 1986

background for what has in most cases to be practical learning on-the-job. It is clear, too, that the overall provision keeps up with technical developments. In addition to the 92 courses listed in Table 6.4 as about computers, 38 of the 68 courses listed under manufacturing processes, control and maintenance are electronics courses, ranging from a variety of basic surveys — introduction to electronic circuits, introduction to mechatronics, etc. — to more specialist courses on sensors and robotics.

The courses are not expensive. A four-month course in adapting a basic database file program to individual firms' stock control systems costs ¥28,000 (about £110) and includes the program disk and rental of an NEC computer for groups of four to six students. (It might, of course, be subsidized by the manufacturer.) A three-month course in workshop safety regulations for foremen and safety committee representatives costs ¥9,000 (£45). A three-month course in the basics of continuous casting — one of the 69 courses offered by the Iron and Steel Junior Technical College — costs less than half that. Six month courses in opt-electronics, industrial robotics, adhesion techniques, finite element analysis or plastics forming techniques run at £200–250.

As to the quality of these courses, it is difficult to make overall judgements. The intending consumer can only judge from the experience of others and the reputation of the course provided. The Ministry of Labour has no content-vetting system for determining the eligibility of courses for subsidy; the regulations require only that the courses should be of 3–12 months in duration, should deal with one of a specified list of subjects, and that, on the recommendation of prefectural authorities (to which applications have first to be made) the Minister of Labour considers them 'suitable'. Only one course has so far been rejected — or rather, its proposer was 'administratively guided' into withdrawing it, because it seemed obviously designed as a housewives' leisure course rather than something employers should sponsor. A certain check is kept on the general character of the organizations offering courses, at least when any misleading advertisements are brought to the Ministry's notice. (The 1984 Vocational Training Act recommends that all enterprises should appoint a qualified Training Guidance Officer. One commercial firm which has created a correspondence course for training such officers claimed that the Ministry was proposing soon to make the appointment of such an officer compulsory — an intention which the Ministry firmly denies. Discussion proceeds as to whether this misrepresentation will amount to a reason for considering the course not 'suitable' when the vetting process takes place at the end of the year.)

There is, however, a formal vetting procedure operated by the Ministry of Education which does have specialist committees examining course content. This, however — another typical expression of the arm's-length relationship between the world of disinterested learning which is the Ministry of Education's preserve, and the world of money-grubbing industry — is limited to courses run by non-commercial bodies: schools and colleges and professional associations, some, like the Japan Shorthand Writers' Association, originally set up by the Ministry to run a professional competence test with which the correspondence course is associated.

There are 169 courses operated by 42 agencies on the list currently approved under this procedure. They include a number of general cultural-interest courses in music, gardening, calligraphy etc., but also a certain number of professional courses, such as one of the rare university initiatives, a metallurgy course run by the mining department of Akita University, a four-month training course run by the Japan Management School, and an 'enterprise health diagnostic course' run by the Japan Enterprise Management College. (This trains employees of large firms to be part-time consultants for the Small and Medium Enterprise Agency's Consultancy Service — a service which yields for the consultants' employers the important side benefit of discovering potentially useful sub-contractors.)

For these courses the Ministry collects statistics. In 1985 a quarter of their registered students were taking general cultural offerings, with an average of 1,137 students per course. Thirty-six per cent were on business courses with an average of 1,048 students and 39 per cent on technical courses with an average per course of 1,506 students (Kakushu 1988, p. 88).

It will be obvious from Table 6.5, however, that the private sector is at least as important as, and in the technical fields more important than, the public sector in correspondence course provision. In the non-commercial sector, there are three major providers of technical training incorporated as formal education institutions — the Japan Institute of Vocational Training which is supported by public funds, and two private colleges, the College for Industrial Efficiency (Sangyō Nōritsu Daigaku, also known in English as Sanno College), a college founded in 1922 by Japan's then equivalent of Britain's Industrial Society, and thirdly the steel industry's junior college. Between them they provide 30 per cent of the technical courses. Half of the other non-profit-making courses come from two organizations supported by employers — the Japan Centre for Vocational Education

(106 companies pay subscriptions of up to £200 a year) and the Japan Management Association (Nihon Nōritsu Kyōkai), which has 1,700 corporate members who pay double that sum. Forty per cent of the technical courses, and nearly a half of all courses, come from commercial firms and presumably bring in their sellers some profit.

Universities and colleges in the formal education system by and large confine their correspondence work to prolonged versions of their Arts and Social Science degree courses. Their involvement in the provision of special-purpose short courses suitable for the Ministry of Labour's list — especially of the national university engineering faculties which one might expect to be involved — is minimal; the Akita University mining course in the Ministry of Education's list may, indeed, be the only one. The point about the arm's-length relation between university and industry has already been made.

COURSES, TESTS, QUALIFICATIONS

One essential condition for the popularity of these courses has yet to be mentioned. A large number of them prepare their corresponding students for a national qualifying examination or skill test. Students on the Ministry of Education's approved courses were asked their motive in taking the courses. Forty-five per cent were taking them for fun, or their cultural improvement, or the chance to earn a bit extra by making a hobby profitable, etc. (It will be remembered that a lot of the Ministry-approved courses were of this sort.) The other replies were:

It is necessary for my work	17%
To get a qualification	31%
Hoping to get a job, change jobs	7%

'To get a qualification' will probably evoke in a British reader the picture of someone bent on occupational advancement. Those who have got a new skill and a qualification to prove it seek to draw a rent on that skill by finding a new job either within or outside their present place of employment. Some of those who are seeking qualifications through correspondence courses in Japan are also doing that. Shorthand-writers, for example, who can climb up from fifth grade to first grade qualification, can then be put on court work and local government work, probably at some enhancement of their salary if they are employees of a shorthand firm, and certainly at some enhancement of their job opportunities if they are freelance.

But the bulk of this qualification-taking is not of that sort at all. Most of the people taking examinations of the State or other public bodies are doing so primarily at their employer's suggestion or insistence — because the law, or a customer, or a quality assurance association representing customers, says that he has to have someone — or many people — with that qualification on his books. The next chapter will deal with this qualification system. Suffice it to say here that it is far more extensive in Japan than in Britain. All countries have a range of jobs which they will not let anyone do unless they have a qualification which provides some guarantee against their inflicting damage on the public — pharmacists, airline pilots, people in charge of explosives and boilers. Japan's singularity lies in:

A. Not entrusting the qualifying process to educational institutions or professional bodies.

B. Extending the definition of the 'public interest' which justifies insistence on qualifications to cover a very wide range of competences.

One example will suffice to illustrate the way in which legislation and administrative initiative can be used to promote industrial efficiency (more fully described in Dore 1981).

In the late 1970s, and with special urgency after the Iranian revolution, the nation's dependence on imported oil was seen as a crucial national economic weakness. Energy conservation became an important national objective. MITI drafted and the Diet passed a 'Law concerning the rationalization of the use of energy'.

All plants in manufacturing, mining and utilities which annually consume more than 3,000 kilolitres' equivalent of oil, gas or solid fuels or 12m kWh of electricity were designated 'listed heat control plants' or 'listed electricity control plants' respectively — or both if they fulfilled both criteria. (The threshold figures were chosen as the points at which there is a kink in the Lorenz curve linking cumulative numbers of factories to proportions of energy consumed — the point beyond which further lowering of the limits would lead to a big increase in the number of plants covered and only a smaller increase in the total volume of energy.) The total number of plants listed at the end of 1980 was about 3,000 — 2,300 for heat, 2,200 for electricity. Together they consumed about 70 per cent of industry's total energy consumption.

Listed factories are required by the law (fine for non-compliance a little under £1,000) to have qualified energy managers — either heat managers or electricity managers or both, depending on their listing. Their number varies depending on the scale of the plant: four heat managers, for instance, in a plant which uses over 100,000 kl.o.e. per annum (unless it is an electricity generating plant, in which case only two.) The function of these energy managers is to seek 'conscientiously . . . to rationalize and improve the use of fuels' (and the factory owner is required to 'give due respect to' their advice). They also have to keep detailed records of all fuel use and of the nature, capacity loading, energy consumption rating, structural modification, etc. of every piece of energy-using equipment in the plant.

MITI directly organized the syllabus and the qualification which determines what an energy manager is. It set up a panel of experts (paid very modest per diems) to draw up the curriculum and set the examinations (held once a year in ten local centres).

There are no pre-requisites for taking the examination and gaining the qualification. They are open to anyone. In practice nearly everyone who enters is an employee, sent by his employer, in the first instance to fulfill legal requirements, but, in a lot of firms which have many more qualified people than the law requires, also as a means of encouraging competence — there were still a little over 3,000 people taking one of the examinations in 1985, although the 3,000 firms involved must long since have got their required stock of energy managers on their books.

Correspondence courses are organized by the Energy Conservation Centre — a quango set up jointly by MITI (using some of its famous Bicycle Racing Fund money) and industry. There are also eight-day courses (two days a week over four weeks) and four-day revision courses held in various centres. Pass rates in 1980, the first year, were 45 per cent for the heat certificate, down to 32 per cent in 1985. The electricity examination is even tougher; 24 per cent passes in 1980, 19 per cent in 1985.

There is an alternative route for more senior people who already have (together with three years' relevant work experience), a tertiary-level engineering training and one of a number of other national certificates: for heat management, for instance, boiler and turbine technician's licence; mechanical, chemical and metallurgical engineering technician's licence; qualified vocational instructor in mechanical engineering licence; and so on. They can attend an intensive six-day course, followed by a one-day examination. Pass-rates are a little higher here: 70 per cent for heat and 48 per cent for electricity in 1985. Four hundred people took one or the other course.

Energy-conservation attracted a good deal of attention as a national objective, but the principle of official compulsion in the pursuit, sometimes of safety, sometimes of efficiency, is widely applied. In one firm of 88 employees there were a total of 24 holding 37 currently valid licences or course completion certificates. Most of them were required by national, prefectural or city regulations — e.g., pollution-control certificates (one for liquid emissions, one for atmospheric); boiler maintenance certificates, crane-slingers' certificates, dangerous materials handlers' certificates, liquid organic chemicals handling cetificate, forklift truck drivers' certificate. Others were not legally compulsory but were encouraged by organizations such as the local Industrial Safety Association — transport safety supervisor's certi- ficate, press-shop supervisor's certificate. Some, finally, were certificates designed to provide encouragement to individuals to improve the level of competence they bring to their work — a certificate of successful completion of a course in heat treatment; a national certificate in metal plating.

In another factory of 500 employees where each department was required to send in plans for its annual training programme, the 1985 plans included 80 people getting one of 30 different kinds of certificate or qualification. There seems to be considerable variation in the extent to which firms give their employees incentives to take correspondence courses and skill tests. The only data found is a survey of 103 firms (no information on the original sample size or the character of the firms) carried out by the publisher of the main guide to qualifications (Kokka 1982). It concerned specifically help for acquiring qualifica- tions. Eighteen firms formally undertook — by promulgated policy — to cover the expenses involved in actually taking tests; 28 had no formal policy but covered expenses in practice; 27 gave 'a certain amount of help'. Thirteen limited their help to giving time off. For the necessary study preparation, however, just over half the firms said that they paid the full cost of correspondence courses; 12 said that they paid for attendance at special training schools or universities; 32 that in some way they provided tuition, either from inside our outside the firm.

ENTERPRISE-OPERATED QUALIFICATION SYSTEMS

A number of firms have for some time had internal skill tests of their own, some of which they extend to sub-contractors — one domestic appliance firm, for example, requires all employees of sub-contractors working on its sub-assembly work to have passed a soldering test. The 1984 revision of the Vocational Training Act allowed the Ministry of Labour to give formal recognition to the internal skill-testing provisions of private firms. It is not clear that this recognition confers on the firm any advantage beyond the satisfaction of enterprise pride, though it probably makes more automatic and generous grants under the Ministry's training subsidy scheme. The first firm to receive this recognition, Nihon Denso, a large automobile parts maker with some 32,000 employees, has contributed a description of its internal programme to a training magazine (ND 1986). The following is a summary:

The firm was founded in 1949 and in 1953 entered into a licensing agreement with the West German firm Robert Bosch. Their contacts brought knowledge of the German Meister certification system, which some of their managers came much to admire. They had started their own three-year apprentice school in 1956, and the start of Japan's State skill testing and certification system in 1959 coincided with the first graduation class. So all 140 of them were encouraged to take one of the tests.

The process snowballed. Those who had passed the tests taught others. Some formal classes were started. There was strong social pressure encouraging people to take the tests, and the uncertified felt small.

They had had a skill-grading system which contributed bonus elements to the wage since 1959 but it was not entirely satisfactory — it did not command universal respect. Also, the increasing numbers of workers who had successfully passed the tests wanted to see certificate ownership reflected in the skill-grading system. This was formally done through changes in regulations in 1964.

But this led to problems. Some of the skills used in ND were explicitly covered in the Ministry's skill-testing system and others were not. So some did and others did not have the chance of earning extra money. In fact, only about 20 per cent of job functions were covered. So the firm started its own test in 1972, beginning with electrical assembly. In about two years they had covered nearly every job in the factory at a level roughly equivalent in difficulty in the Grade 2 tests of the Ministry system. Then in 1976–7 they moved on to do Grade 1 Standards.

In 1979 Aichi Prefecture established its own Skill Evaluation

System to encourage in-firm skill tests, and the ND test system was incorporated. This meant simply that those who were successful got certificates signed by the Prefectural Governor, which looked better, framed on the wall of their sitting room. Under the new 1984 provisions they have put up their electrical assembly test and four others for national recognition — for adoption as a part of the Ministry of Labour's national system.

Tests follow the national pattern; they all have a written section and a practical section. There are no formal educational requirements for the skill tests, but eligibility does depend on having a year's experience for Grade 2, and rather longer for Grade 1. All test taking is voluntary, and employees are charged (¥4,000 for Grade 2, ¥6,000 for Grade 1: £18 and £27 respectively) for taking the test. There is, however, a subsidy of ¥400 per hour (£1.80 — about two-thirds of the legal minimum wage) for time spent practising for the tests. Skill test records are taken account of in promotion decisions.

There is a total of 219 internal tests which, with the state tests as well, cover the whole range of skills used in the factory. There is a review committee for each test which meets once a year to consider any changes required by new technology or any abnormalities in the pass rate.

The Nihon Denso tests have a number of common elements. For example, five subjects are a compulsory part of the written section of every one of the 29 Grade 2 tests:

Quality control (7 hours of instruction)
Health and Safety (3 hours)
The Toyota Just-in-time system (5 hours)
Nihon Denso Products (3 hours)
Mechanical Drawing (4 hours)

Others, like elements of mechanics (3 hours), basic material qualities (4 hours), etc., are common to a range of tests like fractional hp motor assembly, radiator assembly, IC component assembly, etc., but not to the tests for storekeeper or wastewater drain attendant. Exemption can be gained for the written test by attending courses laid on at the factory for an average of 63 hours on ten Sundays during the year — with internal tests of each of the modules of the course.

The Personnel Director has kindly made an estimate of the cost of this system to the firm:

— The 30 curriculum-revision, test-setting committees have about ten members meeting for ten hours a year. That makes approximately £21,000 for 3,000 hours.

— The allowances for test takers' own-time study and practice (£1.80 an hour) amount to ¥90m or £410,000.

— Against these items is to be set the income from test fees of approximately £45,000.

Nihon Denso is obviously an exceptional company: the £410,000 spent on compensation for training associated with these tests is only about one-ninth of the total ¥800m paid out as out-of-hours study subsidies — a sum equivalent to 2 million hours, or 62 hours a year per employee.

THE WORKER: COMMITMENT, INVOLVEMENT

How many of Japan's workers lead this sort of training-intensive worklife, and how enthusiastic do they have to be about their job to take part in these various kinds of training activity? Nihon Denso provides incentives: ¥400 per hour for out-of-hour training, together with the linking of qualifications with (marginal) pay boosts. In general, however, there is rarely any formal recognition in enterprise reward systems of qualifications gained either inside or outside the firm. With a newly acquired and attested skill, a man or woman might be assigned to a different job, but new jobs do not necessarily mean higher salaries, only, possibly, a faster movement up the scale. In the sample of 103 firms mentioned earlier (Kokka 1982) only thirteen firms said they had any link between qualification earning and basic pay grades. A third said that they gave some additional bonus in the monthly salary — though the majority only for specific qualifications (such, presumably, as the ones of which the firm is legally required to employ as possessor). Nineteen firms gave a one-off congratulatory gift of money, and fifteen said that they took qualifications into account when they were taking promotion decisions. The general disjunction between qualification and reward systems applies in the lifetime-employment sector even at the highest levels. Technologists who have been sent by the firm to take a PhD in a foreign university are liable to become irked and disaffected when they discover the discrepancy between their foreign friends' expectation that their career would now make a quantum leap ahead, and the reality — that they may have some difficulty after a couple of years' absence in recovering their position in the promotion stakes.

The material incentives for self-initiated and self-sustained study are, in other words, not great. Even Nihon Denso's incentive payment

106

for self-study was balanced by the charge levied for taking the tests, and the incentive payment itself was well below ordinary wages, let alone overtime rates. It is apparent that material incentives need a lot of supplementation by loyalty and social pressures to keep up the required level of learning activity. In Sample I, 58 per cent of the firms said that they ran courses out of working hours — mainly on Sundays. A third gave days off in lieu (in theory, at least; in many firms employees do not even take their full entitlement of normal holiday). A little over a third paid an allowance on the same lines as Nihon Denso.

Table 6.6 Work-related study programmes: a questionnaire survey

	Private Rlwys	Metal Engrng	Chemicals	Electrical	All
Number of firms in sample	7	10	18	15	50
Number of worker respondents	388	414	470	783	2,055
	%	%	%	%	%
Is there any study/training programme going on in your workplace? Yes	89	25	82	88	74
(*Question to the Yeses only,*) Do you take part, and if so, Enthusiastically?	14	5	18	19	17
Because it's necessary for your work	44	53	47	51	49
Because you have to?	40	34	32	25	31
(Not involved)	2	7	3	3	3
How much of it is outside working hours					
None of it	48	45	39	22	33
Some of it	14	30	39	33	30
Most of it	15	3	10	24	17
All of it	15	4	4	10	9

Source: Kokumin Seikatsu Centre. '*Kinrosha no yoka ni kansuru kenkyu (A survey of workers' leisure)*, 1986.

Certain clues about the enthusiasm and incentive dimension are given in the report of a survey carried out in March 1985 under trade union auspices (Kokumin Seikatsu 1986). It covered nearly 2,400 people in fifty companies in four industries in the Tokyo area. They were asked to fill out a questionnaire, seal it and return it via their workplace union representative — and thanks to union discipline 87 per cent of them did. Union membership which defines the sample would exclude middle-management and above, but include considerable numbers of university graduates in junior management positions, as well as older technical staff. Table 6.6 summarizes some of the results.

Altogether, three-quarters of the respondents said they were involved in some kind of study/self-improvement programme at work. Most of them showed no great enthusiasm when they were asked whether they took part in these programmes in a positive spirit or not, but the majority said they saw the training as necessary for their work. At least two-thirds said that the training involved some use of their own time, and a quarter said that most or all of it was out of working hours.

That question was specifically about training programmes, not about other after-hours activity such as Quality Circles which might involve a certain amount of explicit learning; they were the subject of a separate set of questions. But it seems that the question about study programmes in 'own-time' was taken to refer to study groups and practice training spilling over after hours in the factory or office. A separate question asked about the frequency with which work demands took up their home time. (So little do people assume an absolute right to go home at the end of formal work hours, that after-work 'own time' is seen as being in a different category from Saturdays and Sundays.) Only a quarter said that study connected with their work, or going to take courses, ate into their leisure life — 20 per cent 'sometimes' and 3 per cent 'frequently'.

COVERAGE

The figures from that survey quoted in Table 6.6 give some indication, also, of the general extent of involvement in training programmes — of *what* constitutes the typical Japanese firm. The simplest summatory statistic is the finding that three-quarters of all the worker respondents were involved in some kind of training activity. There were, however, considerable differences between industries, with very much lower rates in engineering than in chemicals, private railways or electrical firms. This, however, is difficult to interpret since all the sample firms in the last three industries had more than a thousand workers, and those in engineering fewer than 500. Firm size differences may exaggerate the differences between industries here, but the ranking of industries by enthusiasm for training was the same in another Ministry survey. The percentage of firms having no formal training programme (in, apparently, a large sample) were: 4 per cent in utilities, and in banking and insurance, 10 per cent in commerce and in general services, and 23 per cent in engineering.

Another measure of coverage is provided by another large-scale survey carried out by the Ministry of Labour in 1985 and relating to training activities in 1984 (Minkan 1986: 1,795 establishments, an effective response rate of 45 per cent of an intended sample of 4,000 establishments with more than 30 workers in the non-agricultural private sector. Sample 5). An attempt was made to measure the overall proportion of their employees who were involved in one of five types of training activity during the twelve-month reference period. The estimates were as follows:

	Percentage of all employees
Off-the-job training within the firm	27
Courses outside the firm	8
Planned on-the-job training, involving a clear specification of training objectives, timetable and trainer responsibility, and monitoring of training outcomes	12
Assistance for individual self-training (correspondence courses, etc.)	7
Full-salary release from work duties for training purposes	2

LARGE FIRMS AND SMALL

There is a common impression that there is a radical differnce in Japan between the large firms with permanent employment, enterprise unions and all the other characteristics of the so-called 'Japanese employment system', and the small firm sector whose workers have none of the security and privileges offered by the large firms. The former live in what are commonly termed 'internal labour markets' (a phrase which wrongly ignores the difference between internal bidding for vacancies in what can reasonably be called an 'internal labour market', and a system of planned career trajectories and internal postings

109

such as one finds in Japanese firms, as in the British army and civil service). By contrast, it is said, workers in the small firm sector are oriented to the external labour market.

In fact, there is no sharp dichotomy. There is, instead, a spectrum, typically illustrated in the clear correlation of average wages with size of enterprise (with wages in enterprises with over 1,000 workers being over 70 per cent higher than in firms with fewer than 30). There is, perhaps, a kink in the smoothness of the spectrum, a kink dividing the firms which have, from those which do not have, enterprise unions to sanction claims to security of employment. But by and large differences are differences of degree. And so it is with mobility rates, with their close relationship to training. Turnover figures correlate with size of firm — but even the small firms with the higher turnover have lower mobility rates than is common in most industrial countries. The ideal of lifetime employment is held at all levels; in the small-firm sector it is just somewhat more often over-ridden by self-interest. Employers and employees in small firms are more concerned with and involved in external labour markets, but still have systems of seniority wage progression, and employers try to keep and promote long-term employees. Small employers are more likely to look to the external market for the skills they need as an alternative to doing their own training, less certain than employers in the large firms that they will be able to reap the proceeds of any investment they make in their employees' training. But they still say in response to questionnaires that they believe in training and are doing, or plan to do, a lot of it.

It also has to be remembered that over large areas of engineering especially, a very high proportion of small firms exist under the technological umbrella of large firms. The example of Mitsubishi Electric was cited earlier and examples could be multiplied. The transfer of new technologies and new skills from large firm purchaser to small firm supplier is standard practice, and so, also, is the sort of guidance and provision of testing services which keeps the skills of small firm workers up to long-established standards. The importance of these transfer mechanisms is indicated by the fact that it is the focus of a major study of regional economic development in Kumamoto prefecture (Haiteku 1986).

For all these integrating mechanisms, differences in skill levels and in training practices still, of course, remain, but they are, for the reasons explained above, more-or-less differences. There are a number of surveys which reveal them. Firstly, for overall differences in training activity, the labour costs survey (Sample 1) reported manufacturing establishments with more than 1,000 employees to be spending the equivalent of 0.5 per cent of their wage bill on training, those with 30–99 workers, 0.2 per cent. Another survey (quoted in RH 1985: 213) showed, not surprisingly, that firms with 30–99 employees were a good deal less likely than large firms to have a specialized training function in their organization, but still just over half of the firms in that size category did have somebody specifically responsible for training, even if that responsibility was usually combined with other functions.

Secondly, a difference is revealed in the survey which forms the basis of Table 6.7. Small firms' training concerns are more directly geared to the need to prepare for new products or to adopt new processes; they are less concerned with general personnel development — see especially the difference in the item 'training consequent on, or preparatory to, promotion'.

Thirdly, a difference exists in methods. Small firms rely more on external training. The Sample 5 survey gives the breakdown by establishment size of the average figures for worker involvement cited earlier. They allow a comparison between establishments with more

Table 6.7 The emphases of training programmes: differences by size of firm

Type of training considered important	Percentage choosing* that answer among enterprises with:	
	5,000 or more employees	30–99 employees
To adapt to newly adopted techniques or equipment	17	23
To handle the manufacture or sale of new products	12	21
To enable redeployed workers to acquire a new skill	8	4
Training consequent to or preparatory to promotion	39	1
Training up of specialists	16	14
To improve quality of product or service	21	28
Generally to raise standards of efficiency	69	56
No response	1	9

Source: Rodosho (Ministry of Labour), *Koyō Kanri Chōsa (Labour management survey)*, 1984, quoted in RH 1985, Appx. 116
*Multiple choices permitted

than 1,000 and those with 30–99 workers. The former firms had 30 per cent of their employees involved in in-house, off-the-job training, the latter 24 per cent. For planned on-the-job training the figures were 18 per cent and 8 per cent. But by contrast, the smaller establishments had had 11 per cent and 3 per cent of employees respectively going on outside courses or receiving paid release from work duties, compared with larger ones' 3 per cent and 0.2 per cent.

Fourthly, it may well be that the larger firms, being able to cream off the labour market, and more likely to have loyal lifetime workers, are better able to evoke self-directed training efforts from their employees. That seems, at least, a plausible explanation of the final size difference shown in the same survey. Aid for self-development was said by the large establishments to have been given to 10 per cent of their employees, by the smaller 30–99 establishments to only 5 per cent.

There are a number of special provisions in the system of subsidies for enterprise training which favour small and medium enterprises (legally defined as firms with fewer than 300 employees, or capitalized at less than ¥100m.) For example, 'training to acquire specialist knowledge or skill' and 'training to aid adaptation to new technology' can be subsidized in large firms only for workers over 40. In SMEs workers aged 25–40 are also eligible. SMEs can claim up to half of the cost of eligible in-house training programmes and two-thirds of course fees for employees sent for training outside the firm; large firms can claim only one-third and one-half respectively.

The subsidy system is relatively new, but as more firms master the fearsome bureaucratic formalities involved in applying for grants, it is plausibly expected that there will be a steady increase in training consortia organized by, or on behalf of small firms, the more so because of the clustering tendency, both in traditional industries (corduroy weaving in several hundred small firms in Hamamatsu, ginghams woven by a similar cluster in Nishiwaki, domestic ceramic ware in Seto, etc.), and in modern ones like the concentration of printed circuit board makers in the Kanagawa and Kyoto areas for example. Add to this that these clusters are organized into local co-operatives which are the channel for a variety of subsidy measures under programmes to modernize declining or threatened industries, which programmes often have a training element.

CONCLUSION

If one were to single out just one salient point from the detail presented in this chapter, the one to choose for a British audience would probably be this: by such criteria as training expenditure and man-hours in formal off-the-job training, Japanese firms would come rather badly out of any international comparison. Where they do seem to be distinctive is in the way they motivate the efforts of individuals to learn in order to gain in competence (competence rather than self-marketability). Also in the way training departments interpret their role as primarily to facilitate and catalyse such efforts.

7

Standards and qualifications

Nihon Denso, described in the last chapter, is an exceptionally skill-minded, training-minded firm. But in its general assumptions about the importance and purpose of skill tests it is typically Japanese.

A very great deal of effort is devoted in Japan to defining standards of competence in various occupations. Much time is devoted to running formal tests of the extent to which individuals meet those standards.

A very high proportion of that testing was established, and is maintained, for the purpose of raising the efficiency level of those who already have jobs, and of the organizations in which they work (a process the Japanese call *reberu-appu* — levelling up). The two other interests commonly involved — the interests of the individuals in improving their marketability, and the social interest in improving the efficiency of the labour market by refining its signalling system — are relatively minor considerations.

What that means is this: Japanese welders (or, as they would be more likely to describe themselves, Japanese company employees who do a lot of welding) take a lot of skill tests. (They have to retake them every three years in fact.) They do so for a variety of reasons — partly for their own personal satisfaction and pride (remember that they live in a society in which there is a great respect for skills), partly, sometimes, in small firms because they would be that much better placed to get a new job if their present firm went bankrupt or they quarrelled with the boss. But usually the overwhelming reason is because their employer wants them to. And he wants them to because of his own quality-consciousness and because he wants orders from quality-conscious customers. The idea that once they have got the certificate they can go looking for another and better job is not present in the minds of most of the test-takers. And the Association which runs the tests is not much concerned with making it easy for employers recruiting from the labour market to tell a good welder from an indifferent one.

Given the widespread nature of the lifetime employment assumption, the emphasis on loyal commitment which it entails, and its corollary that employers tend initially to look a bit askance at those seeking to change jobs, it is obvious why such an emphasis makes sense. It is only in the more mobile sectors of the labour market — in the construction industry, for example — that getting a qualification in order to change to a better job is at all common.

SKILL TESTING: THE WELDING EXAMPLE

As an example of skill testing in the dominant life-employment sectors of manufacturing, welding might, indeed, be a good place to start. Or even more narrowly the welding of aluminium and other non-ferrous metals (Keikin 1986a, 1986b).

The Japan Light Metal Welding and Construction Association was started in 1962 as an off-shoot of the Japan Welding Engineering Society (which now specializes in ferrous metals). In March 1986 it had a membership of 127 firms and 6 kindred associations, plus 203 individual members — either individual employees of member firms or university engineers. Membership fees range from over £4,000 for firms with over 1,000 employees and a representative on the Association's council, to £450 for firms with fewer than 30 employees. Individuals can join for £35.

The Association carries out a wide range of activities of the kind performed in Britain by industry research associations — cooperating with MITI's Japan Industrial Standards organization, and ISO committees, providing technical information, holding research seminars under the auspices of its various technical committees (non-destructive testing, welding automation, aluminium ships, etc.). Together with its German and American counterparts it has organized technical conferences and was playing host to the fourth International Conference on Aluminium Weldments in 1987. (The organizers remarked that their invitations had drawn no response from the British Welding Institute or the UK Aluminium Federation.)

But one of its major activities, and its main *raison d'être*, is its skill-testing and certification system. Test fees brought in about £300,000 of its £600,000 1985 operating expenses.

Separate tests cover a variety of skills — welding edge-to-edge, with and without backing, with aluminium strip or with titanium strip, pipe welding, etc. For each test there is a written exam and a practical. The practical test is conducted with impressive thoroughness. A complex system of punch-marks and indelible ink is designed to ensure that all strips cut off for destructive testing are identifiable and that no sleight of hand can substitute a perfect weld for a candidate's imperfect test-piece — or vice-versa. After visual inspection the test pieces are sent to the Association's laboratory. One strip is folded across the weld one way, a second strip the other, and the weld is microscopically examined. These test procedures conform strictly to a JIS standard (Z3811: Methods of skill testing for aluminium welding and the standards to be applied) which is said to be of roughly equivalent rigour to the British BS4872.

Tests are held both in company premises and in facilities such as national or prefectural technical schools. At one Saturday test session in the northern prefectural town of Fukushima some thirty candidates came mostly from small firms, most of which did contract fabrication for the local railway carriage works. Altogether, 76 test sessions were held up and down the country in 1985, candidate numbers ranging from a dozen to over 100. The number of tests taken was 4,423 — by 2,947 people. The overall pass rate was 68%, though 76% passed at least one test. There is, however, a total of only about 10,000 certificated aluminium welders in the country since the tests have to be frequently retaken.

The licence (with photograph) is valid for a year. It is renewed for two more years against an employer's certificate affirming that the licensee has actually been doing the work for which he was tested. Every third year the test has to be taken again.

The tests are mostly held on Saturdays, the examiners being drawn from a panel of twenty veteran members of the society (some from business firms, some from university engineering departments and some from government departments) who are paid a very modest £40 for their day's work. The cost to the candidates — or, usually, their employers — varies according to the complexity of the test and the subsequent analysis, and the cost of materials, from £30 to as much as £200 for special pipe work.

The Association also runs two other types of tests for individuals; one for X-ray testing of welds, and the other for supervisors of welded structure work (the last at three levels, the top level requiring a good deal of metallurgical and legal as well as quality-testing knowledge). Fifty took one type of the former in 1985 (with a pass rate of 56%) and 34 the latter (pass rate 68%). The Association is preparing a new set of tests for ultrasonic weld inspection to be promulgated in 1987.

There are textbooks published by the Association for all these courses, and short courses are run at various centres in different parts of the country, though the uptake seems to be low; most people manage with a textbook for the book work and practical training in the workplace. The welding practice course, which lasts for five days, was attended by 109 people at the 9 centres at which it was held in 1985.

Factory certification is a newer — and lesser — activity of the Association, started in 1980. Only four or five factories apply each year for Quality Assurance certification of the type practised by Lloyds or the MoD in Britain. Perhaps strangely for a country with such an emphasis on group activities, the Association concentrates primarily on individual certification.

In spite of the scale of its operations, the Association does not have a monopoly over tests for light metal welding in Japan. There are three other testing bodies all of which, however, conform in their testing methods and pass grade criteria to the same JIS standard (Z 3811). They are differentiated according to type of work. The Maritime Association runs tests specifically for welding on large ships, especially LP gas transporters where high quality welds are required. The Shipping Bureau of the Ministry of Transport runs tests for more general shipping work, and the Ministry of Labour's skill-testing centres run tests for boiler-making work and high-pressure containers. The Non-destructive Testing Association also runs tests in radiography inspection procedures in parallel with the Aluminium Association's, and there are arrangements for mutual recognition of each other's tests.

So much for the minority activity of welding light metals. The body concerned with ferrous welding — the Japanese Welding Engineering Society — operates on a much bigger scale. Its annual operating budget was, in 1985, of the order of £12 million. Its outreach has steadily grown since the vanguard of 29 welders took its first test in 1949. The number of candidates for one of its 10 different types of craft tests in 1985 was 98,000, of whom 76 per cent passed. Another 3,500 took its technician's or supervisor's certificate test — only 47% of them passed. The total number holding valid certificates was around 190,000 craftsmen and 22,000 technicians in March 1986 (Yōsetsu 1986a, 1986b).

SKILL-TESTING BODIES

It will be noted that these certificates of welding competence are given

117

not by associations of welders, but by associations of people who employ welders.

In Britain, with an older, more slowly evolving system of skill certification, the dominant pattern remains some form of peer approval. The granting of qualifications is very largely the privilege of occupational and professional associations — associations of the individuals who own certain skills and are in the business of selling their skilled labour, or of selling services using those skills, in the market.

In Japan, by contrast, it lies much more in the hands of those who *buy*, or represent those who buy, skills or the services which use those skills — associations of employing organizations in the case of the welders, the state in many other cases.

Thus, the competence of a British craftsman was originally attested solely by his peers' willingness (on condition of a suitable period of time-serving apprenticeship) to admit him to the body of practitioners and to a share in any monopoly power that body of practitioners might have — once given, through guild charters, by local potentates, later through arrangements with employers. Only slowly have the customers come to be involved — at first the individual firms where the apprenticeship was carried out; for the last twenty years through tripartite training boards — and only slowly and partially has the customer's interest in objective testing of competence had any impact on certification procedures.

The public interest in reassurances of occupational competence varies, of course, with the occupation. *Caveat emptor* may be good enough for buying the services of a bricklayer, but not for buying more arcane, unjudgeable and possibly dangerous services like those of a doctor or a lawyer. Even in such cases, however, the weak states of earlier centuries could not do much better than put the professional associations on their honour; to grant monopoly charters on condition of promises of conscientious service, Hippocratic oaths and so on. These paleo-corporatist arrangements (as one might call them to distinguish them from the neo-corporatist arrangements of modern tripartite bodies like the MSC) persist today. The crust of tradition is not easily broken, as the Monopolies Commission report on the professions showed in 1977. It is still the BMA which controls the certification of doctors, though the Ministry of Health and the NHS have steadily increased their influence on how that control is used.

The situation is very different in Japan. The crust of tradition has twice been broken in major social upheavals, major bouts of institutional renewal. The first was under the aegis of the strong state which

118

emerged from the Meiji Restoration in the nineteenth century, the second under the infinitely stronger and bureaucratically more competent state of the 1940s and 1950s. The development of national certification systems for the major professions — lawyers, doctors, pharmacists, etc. — certification by the state acting as watchdog for the customers — belongs to the first of those periods. The extension of the principle to a wide range of industrial skills belongs to the second.

THE RISE OF THE TRAINING INTEREST

The contrast between Britain and Japan has so far been drawn only in terms of two major actors in the certification business — the professional-association sellers of skills, and the state or other association of customers. There is, of course, a third major actor in modern societies: the professional trainers.

With the development of schools and colleges teaching occupational skills, the other two bodies involved increasingly delegate to them — at their urgent insistence, usually — the right to define and indentify competence. University degrees and graduation certificates come to entitle their holders to exemptions or partial exemptions from professional examinations and, where they exist, from state examinations. British driving schools have not yet been given the right to conduct their own driving test as an alternative to the state's, but the definition of what constitutes a good pharmacist or nurse has long since been left to the schools that train them.

The pressures behind that process are as strong in Japan as they are in Britain. It is, of course, a problematic process. Training institutions have a strong interest in making sure that a high proportion of their students qualify — both from kindly concern and because they want to attract students next year. That strong interest may make them less concerned with standards — or with adapting standards to changing contemporary needs — than the ultimate customers would like.

This discussion provides a framework for saying what is distinctive about the Japanese system of skill testing as compared with that of Britain. One might summarize as follows:

1. Central and local government plays a much greater, and occupational associations play a much smaller role in setting and enforcing standards.

2. The definition of the public interest which permits public authorities to *insist* on state-certified competence is a good deal wider, including for instance, to take the example given in the last chapter, the national need to conserve energy or to reduce pollution.

3. Beyond the sphere of compulsion, the national interest in economic success has been seen to justify government leadership in attempting to define levels of competence in an exemplary way — setting standards for efficient milling and grinding and sausage-making in order to help customers to insist on efficiency. (Much as the same shared national interest in economic efficiency, and in the nation's exporters' reputation, justified government inspection of export cloth in 1919 and of export bicycles in the late 1940s.)

4. These two aspects of government action have left private associations with a lesser role in certification, but where private associations do play a role, associations of the organizations which employ skilled people are relatively more important than associations of the skilled people themselves.

5. Although the tendency to delegate certifying functions to training institutions is apparent in Japan as in Britain, it is rather more strongly resisted in Japan.

6. Where new training needs are identified as a result of new technology or new social problems, the Japanese do invest in new training institutions. But they are also more likely than the British to use the Exchequer-cheaper alternative of setting standards and establishing a testing system as a means of catalysing private training efforts.

QUALIFICATION EXAMINATIONS RUN BY CENTRAL GOVERNMENT

The new Ad Hoc Committee on Educational Reform has recently taken stock of the various types of qualifications which are controlled by central government departments. According to its listings the total numbers are of the following order:

Type of qualification	*Number of Branches*	*Exams**
Qualifications legally required as a condition for exercising certain professional functions (pilot's license, atomic power technician, dental technician, hairdresser, etc.)	128	146
Qualifications legally required as a condition for assuming certain self-descriptions (Candidate Accountant, Registered Engineer, Health Visitor, Dietician, Sewage Superintendent, Master Cleaner (of clothes), etc.)	29	31
Qualifications required for appointments to government posts (Primary School Teacher, Technical Superintendent of Waste Disposal Works, Home Counsellor for Working Youth, etc.)	23	23
Qualifications designed to certify and encourage high levels of occupational performance	306	563

*In some branches there is more than one examination. There are two grades for each of the Ministry of Labour's skill tests — e.g. for First-class Well-borer and Second-class Well-borer. Some have more — e.g. three for the Ministry of Communcation's wireless telegraphy and five for the Ministry of Education's shorthand writing tests.

AN EXAMPLE: HAIRDRESSING

Hairdressing may be given as an example of the sort of occupation which most countries do not consider to require the same sort of treatment for qualifying purposes as piloting an aeroplane. The Japanese barber and hairdresser, however, will have gone through a two-year course at a school very like the one whose finances were described in Chapter 5. There he or she will have attended lectures and done practical work on volunteers from 9 a.m. until mid-afternoon. Most pupils have a helper's job in a hairdressing saloon for the rest of the day where they join what is usually a hierarchy of practitioners — starting as the one who sweeps and tidies and looks after hot towels and dresses the customer in his protective smock, progressing to combing, shaving edges, and preparing the customer for shampooing, and finally being allowed to cut the hair of friends of the proprietor, but only, probably some time after graduation.

The classroom study covers quite a wide field, and only those who pass the two-hour multiple choice written paper are eligible to take the other half of the qualifying examination, the practical. The written paper is set by a prefectural committee, but to a standard national syllabus and to examination guidelines set by a central Ministry of Health committee, so that there is little local variation. The Fukushima 1986 examination, for instance, was divided into nine parts. The first part on the legal structure began by asking which was the correct statement of the following three:

1. The Environmental Laws comprise the Epidemic Diseases Law, the Immunization and Vaccination Law, and the Tuberculosis Prevention Law.

2. The Public Hygiene Laws comprise the Preventative Hygiene Law, the Environmental Hygiene Law, and other laws relating to public health.

3. The Labour Hygiene Laws comprise the Mental Health Law, the Hot Springs Law and the Law concerning Dieticians.

A later question wants to know whether practising as a hairdresser without a hairdresser's license made one liable to a fine of up to ¥2,000, up to ¥5,000 or up to ¥10,000.

The next section on anatomy and physiology asks, for instance, that the candidate should spot the error in a set of statements: that a healthy adult has six to eight thousand white corpuscles per cubic millimetre of blood; that an adult's blood makes up a fifth of bodyweight, or that haemoglobin has the function of carrying oxygen in the bloodstream. The sterilization section requires the ability to tell percents from permills and to tell the difference between alkaline soap, formalin and sodium nitrate solution. Then comes infectious diseases (differences between bacteria and viruses, whether it was Koch who identified typhus, Hansen who mastered cholera or Shiga who elucidated dysentery, etc.), public hygiene, the elements of dermatology, and basic physics and chemistry (what conducts heat and electricity, what volt and calorie are measures of, whether it is true that the PH index is a measure of the density of hydrogen ions, etc.). Finally, there are two alternative sections: basic barbering theory and basic hairdressing theory. They require the candidate to assess the truth of statements like: razoring should in principle be done on the slant at an angle of 45 degrees to the lie of the hair, or: a maypole curl starts from the root of the hair and leaves the hair ends on the outside.

It is hard to imagine how eighteen-year-olds with twelve years of general education already behind them could spend two years learning to pass an examination of this sort, but it may be harder — especially for people from more pragmatic and philistine cultures — to under- stand why they should be expected to. One not irrelevant answer is that it contributes to the sense of professional pride, the sense of belonging to an honourable and socially useful occupation, on the part of barbers. (Even in areas where a sense of professional pride is irrelevant, such as in driving, written tests are given on the mechanics of cars although the majority of successful candidates will never attempt to repair or recondition their cars themselves. But the prevailing belief is that knowing about how car engines function makes them better drivers.) It is noticeable, at any rate, that there are no public protests from the hairdressing profession at the expense involved — and, as was described in Chapter 5, barbers' voluntary contributions provide important financial support for the schools. Presumably — although the authors did not have a chance to go into this — the desirability of sustaining these voluntary efforts is the argu- ment for having these parts of the examination set by local prefectural committees, rather than set centrally at much lower cost and with lesser difficulty of maintaining national comparability of standards.

It may be argued, in other words, that the importance of these written parts of the tests for manual skills — and the hairdressing pattern is a standard one — is more symbolic than substantive. They are not designed to ensure that every barber remembers who Koch was; only to ensure that they are aware of the legal framework in which they work, are respectful of their ancestors' work in accumu- lating the knowledge which has provided them with the practical tools of their trade, are receptive to the fruits of possible further progress, and are accustomed to the idea that useful knowledge can be gained by reading and personal inquiry. Those who have had their hair cut in Japan will at least agree that the process produces barbers who are not only deft, conscientious and meticulously hygienic, but also better able than less articulate barbers in other countries to explain the supposed chemical action of the cosmetics they commend, or the structure of the neck muscles they will offer to massage.

LEVELS AND GRADES

A good proportion of the qualifications run by central government are of the kind normally taken by university graduates. Thus, there are two grades of examinations in architecture, run by the Ministry of Construction — to which has been added in 1984 a new qualification — in wooden building construction — on a par with the lower (grade 2) architect's qualification. University graduates need not take the grade 2 examination and can go on to the grade 1 examination after two years' practical experience; graduates of three-year colleges after four years' experience. Those who have been to a building course in a Vocational High School can take a grade 2 examination after three years' experience, and then, four years later, the grade 1. Those without any relevant academic training require seven years' experience before they can take the first grade and another four before they are eligible for full qualification. These examinations, incidentally, are not a walk-over. The 1984 figures were: 51,000 taking the grade 2 examination and 23 per cent passing, with 27,000 taking the parallel wooden construction test and 25 per cent passing. For the higher examination, for which 63,000 entered, the pass rate was only 13 per cent.

MODALITIES

The routes by which the central government intervenes in the qualification process are various. As in the example of the energy manager's licence quoted in the last chapter, one device is to pass a law requiring that certain types of enterprise, engaged in certain types of business or using certain kinds of materials, must employ people with certain qualifications, and then either directly, or through a specially created quango, to create the qualification and subsequently administer the examinations which grant it. A large number of MITI's qualifications are of this type — a wide range of qualifications relating to pollution control, the management of explosives, mine safety, patent law work etc.

A second method, used when the objective is to raise performance standards rather than to deal with an acknowledged public danger or potential source of corrupt practice, is to issue a set of regulations to give official recognition to the right of certain bodies to set standards and test individuals' ability to meet them. Thus, while automobile maintenance is a state qualification of the first type, run by the Ministry of Transport (or, rather, a variety of qualifications of different types and grades — thirteen altogether), bicycle maintenance is dealt with in this second, more indirect, fashion. It is in fact handled by MITI which, in 1979, issued an administrative order, or notification (a *kokuji* which does not require Diet approval, nor is based on legislation) concerning bicycle manufacture and repair. The first clause reads:

In order to raise the quality and efficiency standards of bicycles supplied to the public and to ensure safety in their use, the Minister of International Trade and Industry will give official recognition to those organizations engaged in the testing and certification of knowledge and skill in assembling, inspecting and maintaining bicycles (of those who are engaged in the business of assembling, inspecting and maintaining bicycles), which he deems to deserve encouragement in acknowledgement of their efforts to raise the standards of knowledge and skill applied to the assembling, inspecting and maintaining of bicycles.

The Ministry then guided the industry into creating a non-profit Association to run such tests under its supervision. By 1986 743 people had taken the examination and 559 had passed.

Those figures are hardly indicative of an enthusiastic public response. And it has to be said that the public-policy purpose of some of these civil servant initiatives is not always unalloyed by other considerations — such as the fact that the associations thus created provide pleasant and undemanding post-retirement jobs for civil servants of the Ministry which created them. The bicycle assembly/repair initiative might well be suspected of a substantial input of alloyed motivation, since the National Police Agency has had a similar skill test operating under the aegis of one of *its* particular retirement-haven agencies, the Traffic Control Technology Association, ever since 1954, and it still has a much higher number of candidates for its tests. The MITI association and the TCTA in fact run their practical tests jointly, and only the written parts of the examination are separate.

However, to say that these initiatives often kill two birds with one stone is not to argue that the public-policy bird is always, or even usually, a stuffed one. A good number manifestly fill, and are appreciated as filling, genuine needs. Another of many examples one might take of the use of the same administrative device — the *kokuji* sanctioning the establishment of an association — is the Ministry of Education's initiative in 1965 to set up a Shorthand Writers' Association. It reports annually to the Ministry which in theory scrutinizes its operations to decide whether it should continue to receive recognition as sole certifier of shorthand skills. (The official concerned was, at least, able to lay his hands instantly on the file containing its annual reports, among the several tens of files piled on and around his desk.) The Association has a modest three-person office, a council of sixteen men and three women (nearly half of them graduates of the Diet shorthand training school) and a budget of £150,000. About 6,000 people take one or other of its six grades of test every year, with pass rates ranging from 35 per cent in the lowest grade to 25 in the highest.

The various welding tests described at the beginning of this chapter also have their origin in some kind of officially-inspired arrangement, and the main guide to qualifications lists a number of others: the dog-trainer's certificate run by the Police Dog Association, the concrete technician's certificate run by the Japan Concrete Industry Association, the micrographics technician certificate run by the Japan Microfilm Association, and so on.

THE MINISTRY OF LABOUR SKILL TESTS

The most extensive·system of all is that run by the Ministry of Labour which accounts for the vast majority of the qualifications in the last category listed at the beginning of the chapter — the 306 kinds of 'qualifications designed to certify and encourage high standards of occupational performance'. The tests available range from woodwork machinery maintenance and tyre recapping to the making of tatami and the installation of jacuzzi baths. There are 129 trades altogether, many of which are subdivided by specialty. Well-boring, for instance, has two types of certificates, each with two grades — percussion methods and rotary methods. Metal refining has eight branches depending on whether it is iron, steel, copper or aluminium, and on the type of furnace — crucible, cupola, draw or reverberating. Machining has 25 certificates (or, rather, 50, since each comes in two grades): general lathe work, turret lathes, vertical lathes, CNC lathes, slotting machines, milling machines, machining centres, etc.

For each of the 129 trades there are committees of the central quango, the Japan Vocational Ability Development Association. Their members — who derive more honour/pride than cash from their involvement — are in charge of development of the syllabus for each of the certificates, and may suggest subdivisions of their field when technical change introduces new complications. The press of getting a new certificate established takes about three years, from first proposal, through approval of a draft syllabus (between the JVADA and Ministry of Labour officials), inclusion in the Ministry's budget proposals (by August for the following April), budget approval, elaboration of the syllabus in consultation with the relevant prefectural committees and finally promulgation.

Six new certificates were added in 1986. The press release announcing them was embargoed 'until after the Cabinet meeting of 8 August'. Skill tests are a serious matter; if only for the five-second item, 'approval of changes in administrative regulations' they at least get on the Cabinet agenda. The first paragraph of that release reads:

> The skill test system exists to test the skills of workers according to objective criteria and to publicly attest to the standards attained, thereby providing workers with objectives to strive for, enhancing their motivation to acquire skills, raising the skill levels they attain and consequently their status, and contributing, also, to the development of the national economy.

The six new branches were:

Fabrication of objects using rope (e.g., rope nets for crane slinging)

Preparation, design layout of material for making plates for off-set printing

Fish sausage making (a sub-division of the previously existing 'ham and sausage making')

Curtain wall construction (metallic sheets used on high-rise buildings)

Pressurized concrete pumping (formerly included in 'reinforced concrete construction')

Industrial cleaning (formerly part of 'Building cleaning'), cleaning, involving the use of chemicals, of oil refineries, chemical plants, reservoirs, etc.

The administration of the tests is the work of prefectural committees, and of their test-specific sub-committees. For the lower grade, test papers are set locally (but to the national standard syllabus). There is a written test as well as the practical test for every examination. (Our discussion of the hairdressing syllabus has already commented on the symbolic as well as substantive importance of the written part of these examinations — a reflection of Confucian traditions and a reinforcement, as well as a reflection, of the high level of verbal articulacy of the Japanese population remarked on at the beginning of Chapter 6.) The higher grade examinations (and the single grade in the case of nine trades for which there is no grade division) are administered centrally, and the certificate is signed by the Minister of Labour, not, as with the grade 1 certificate, by the Prefectural Governor. (Both need to get elected, and it does no harm to have your signature decorating thousands of living room and office walls.)

The administrative costs of these testing services are not high. Testees pay ¥2,300, or about £10 for a written examination and about five times that much for a practical. The Ministry of Labour Vocational Training Schools are commonly used as the testing centres for both grades of examination. The ¥¾ bn (£3.5m) which the Ministry spends on the testing system each year, represents only a small part of the training budget. (See Table 4.2. The decline in this budget item is not a trend decline, but the effect of exceptionally high spending in the previous year for a special overhaul programme.)

The Ministry of Labour estimates that 1.3 million people have got test certificates of one kind or another since the system began in 1959.

There is a major difference between this system and the certification system run, e.g. by the City and Guilds in Britain. A high proportion of those taking the British examinations do so from technical colleges and other training institutions as the culmination of some initial, either day-release or full-time pre-employment, training. The external qualification and the course are intimately related. In Japan, this is not so. The courses for 15-year-olds at the Vocational Training Schools described in Chapter 4 are, indeed, designed to train for the grade 2 certificate examination, but these are far from supplying the majority of examinands. The Tokyo metropolitan Vocational Ability Development Association has prepared a statistical breakdown of the 4,060 men and 527 women who took one or the other grade of skill test in the prefecture in 1985. Only 12 per cent had been on any kind of institutional training course at the Vocational Training Schools, and only two per cent at one of the senshu-gakko described in Chapter 5. Twenty-one per cent had at some time been at a Vocational High School on a relevant course. (Nearly double that proportion, however, had been at an ordinary academic high school, and of the 19 per cent of first-test takers who had been to a university, only a half had been in a relevant vocational department.)

It is doubtful, however, whether for most of the test-takers there was any direct institutional link between their attending a vocational training course and their taking the test. For most trades, although one can take the written part of the test in an educational institution, and in some cases that institution's own examinations are accepted as a substitute for the state written test, the practical examination cannot be taken until after one or two year's work experience. In fact, only a little over one per cent of those taking the lower grade examination were under 20 years of age, and only five per cent of them had had less than two years' work experience, 36 per cent less than four. Thirty-eight per cent of those taking this lower grade test were over 30. For the higher grade, indeed, over a quarter of those taking the test were over 40, and fewer than ten per cent had less than eight years' work experience.

The great majority of those taking tests, in other words, were not doing so as the routine culmination of a training course, but getting themselves a qualification which in some way grew out of their work career and ratified skills they had acquired. The last chapter described how a number of large companies encouraged their employees to take these skill tests, as a means of promoting quality-enhancing efficiency. The Tokyo metropolitan figures showed 27 per cent of test-takers to be from enterprises with over a thousand employees. Seventeen per cent were from enterprises with fewer than 10, and nearly a half from those with fewer than a hundred workers.

The other function of these qualifications — as an insurance in case one finds oneself in the labour market looking for another job — is much more likely to influence the latter group of workers, those in the small firms, particularly those in construction: nearly 30 per cent of the Tokyo candidates were taking tests in some kind of construction skill. In the construction industry, where work is more seasonal and workforces more mobile, these skill qualifications almost certainly do have a more important labour-market signal function than in other branches of the economy. The major published guide to qualifications says, for instance, of the architect's qualification, that there are about 611,000 people in Japan with an architect's qualification, first or second class, and only 35,000 freelance architects, so the vast majority must be employees. It goes on: 'having a qualification helps also if you want to change your job. With a qualification, up to the age of 35 or so at least, you can hope in a new job to get paid at your normal age rate, or even better.' (The reference is to the common practice of paying 'mid-career recruits' somewhat less than lifetime employees of the same age.) (Kokka 1986: 539)

NON-OFFICIAL QUALIFICATIONS

As the main guide to qualifications says, in introducing the last 20 of its 800 pages — the section devoted to 'miscellaneous non-official qualifications':

> Non-official qualifications are a field for free competition. Anyone can promulgate a qualification. The fact that you register the title of, say, Real Estate Journalist with the Patent Office and prevent anybody from using the term without authorization does not of itself endow it with any meaning or substance . . . . That people should fall for expensive but worthless pieces of paper may seem strange, but one reason is that people who buy these educational consumer goods called qualifications have no easy means of knowing the quality of what they are buying.
>
> (Kokka 1986: 728)

And it has to be said that the guide itself neither makes any attempt to give an evalution of the courses it lists, nor makes any claims to have vetted its listings and excluded the worthless, though it does print a list of the qualifications offered by bodies which are approved members of the central federation of business education bodies, the Japan Management Association (Nihon Noritsu Kyokai) mentioned in Chapter 6 as running a large number of correspondence courses.

The total list runs to about 140 qualifications, predominantly in the business field. Thirty-seven are listed under accounting, finance and law — specialties like company auditing, investment analysis, financial control, etc. as well as a few miscellaneous skills like word processing and specialist skills like hotel management. Twelve concern personnel management; twenty-one are listed under a rather miscellaneous category: production and sales. Three certify skill in detection work (primarily checking credit-worthiness). Five cover architectural specialties; ten, languages (including Esperanto); fifteen, medical administration and insurance, welfare, counselling, etc. The final fourteen in the miscellaneous category run from English shorthand, proof-reading, and the use of the abacus, to music qualifications run by a subsidiary of the Yamaha piano company, and numerous qualifications in household pet care.

QUALIFICATIONS AND THE EDUCATIONAL SYSTEM: OPEN ACCESS

The way in which schools and colleges seek to 'capture' the qualification process, not always to the larger social benefit, was mentioned at the beginning of this chapter. That process is apparent in Japan, too, in various provisions for exemptions — usually only from the written part of examinations and skill tests — given to those who have completed particular courses. Exemptions in the skill tests for those who have taken courses at the Ministry of Labour Vocational Training Schools are an example. But overall the extent to which this process has advanced is incomparably smaller in Japan than in, for example, Britain. At the professional level — medicine, law, architecture, etc. — it has.hardly advanced at all. It is not difficult to imagine why: once the qualifying function is in the hands of the state it is more likely firmly to stay there than when it is in the hands of a professional body much more prone to delegate to the trainers.

There is another influence of educational institutions on the qualification system — at the entry end. In theory, there is no reason why a professional examination or a skill test should not be open to absolutely anyone. If the test is a good one it will identify competence, and all it certifies is just that competence. If those who lack the necessary background take the test and fail it, that is their affair. Since they pay for it, they inconvenience no-one but themselves. However, appealing though these arguments for complete 'open access' may be, such hardline rationality is rarely practised. It is common (one of the first examples was the forerunner of the BMA in 1851) for qualifying bodies to insist on certain levels of general education as a precondition for being able to enter courses or take tests to qualify professionally. One reason is pressure from the educational authorities who want some institutional recognition of the idea that general education is a good thing.

A high proportion of Japanese tests also have such requirements, though usually in the form that a higher level of general education will reduce the number of years of practical experience required before the test may be taken. In other words practical experience of the occupation in which competence is being tested is the basic requirement: extra education can earn exemptions. There are also a good

131

number of qualifications for which the 'hardline rationality' line holds, access is genuinely open and no entry qualifications are specified, either in terms of experience or years of schooling.

There has, moreover, recently been a move towards the 'hardline rationality' direction. This is unusual, given that it is common in other countries for the entry standards required slowly to escalate over time, particularly in countries like Britain where professional bodies compete with each other for status and for 'pools of talent' defined in terms of general educational achievement. Qualifications which once required O-levels for entry, now require A-levels; those which required A-levels are now likely to ask for a degree. And so on.

Japan has been no exception to this process of escalation in educational requirements as far as job-recruitment is concerned. As a natural result of educational expansion, shop-floor workers, once recruited from middle school, now come from high school; local government clerks come, now, not from high school but from university. But the process seems not much to have affected the qualifying requirements for taking occupational and professional qualifications. And, thanks to the Ad Hoc Commission on Education, there has even been a certain lowering of formal requirements to allow anyone to qualify for anything they are competent to qualify for. At least, there has been a formal declaration of the desirability of moving in that direction, though the actual changes in regulation have been marginal. Graduates of senshu-gakko can now take a grade 2 skill test immediately on graduating, for instance, whereas they formerly had to have a year's work experience. Middle-school leavers can go directly to a grade 1 test after 12 years' work experience, instead of 14!

QUALIFICATION AND STATUS

One other feature of the Japanese qualification system is worth pointing out in view of Britain's recent Review of Vocational Qualifications and the MSC's Working Group's recommendation for a tidying up of Britain's miscellaneous qualifications into five 'levels'.

There are two possible approaches to the business of certifying vocational competence. One is to treat skills as discrete and miscellaneous, infinitely varied in their requirements for mastery and varied, also, in the ways in which they may be combined together in actual occupational roles. The unit breakdown of skills for testing purposes may therefore be allowed to follow the logic of the particular tasks to which they relate. Some, like driving, will require days of training of automatic reflexes, some will require weeks of cerebral learning, some, months of practical experience. Actual occupational roles may call for a wide variety of ways of combining different skills. Individuals may combine the ability to draft machine drawings, to operate a milling machine, to do double-entry bookkeeping, to design houses or to supervise heating systems in all kinds of diverse ways, just as boy scouts collecting proficiency badges may have an infinite number of variations. For certification purposes let the certificates *be* like boy scout badges. Let individuals collect as many as they like, of the kind they like, in combinations which are relevant to the work (the constantly changing, and with technological change increasingly rapidly changing, pattern of work) available to them.

The alternative is the whole-role certification approach, which assumes that the way skills are combined in practice is limited, and the important thing is to certify whether or not a person has acquired one of these 'standard packages' required for standard occupational roles. This is essentially the approach in Britain. There is, indeed, nowadays some recognition that an engineering craftsman may combine a variety of different skills. Those skills may be taught or tested in discrete units, but these are only modules of a larger whole. They have little meaning unless they add up to a definable — conventional — occupational role.

But if one can reach equivalent certified status by combining any six of a dozen modules, fairness demands that each of these modules should be of equal 'worth' — i.e., demanding equal intelligence, effort and time-input. So the modules have to be designed so that each one can be accomplished by a person of average effort levels and in the intelligence band expected for the occupational role in question, in the course of x classroom or practice hours. Never mind the intrinsic requirements for overhauling a diesel engine or operating a grinding machine. If they are such that x hours is too many, then add in something else to make weight. If too few, then skimp a bit on some of the less essential bits.

This second, the contemporary British, way of proceeding is one of the less commonly remarked, but not necessarily less important, of the 'rigidities' in labour markets which are so commonly deplored. It is rigid both in the Procrustean moulds into which the learning and teaching is forced, and in the limited range of combinations of skills which 'whole-role' certification permits. It becomes even more rigid, of course, if all the 'whole-roles' have got to be fitted into a five-level hierarchy as is now proposed in Britain's tidying-up operation.

A lot of Japan's certification is whole-role certification, too, of

133

course — the state examinations for doctors, pharmacists, architects, etc. But for intermediate and lower level skills, the choice of the 'discrete and miscellaneous' approach (except possibly in the Ministry of Labour system where there is a governing presumption that all 'Grade 1' or all 'Grade 2' qualifications are of very roughly equal degrees of mastery) gives much greater flexibility.

The choice of qualification system cannot, of course, be separated from pay systems. Japan puts people on scales which (as in the UK civil service) are primarily geared to their educational status — as middle school, high school, college or university graduate. British pay systems, particularly for manual workers, are tightly bound by skill status. Both are about equally determinate in the sense that life chances are determined early. Although the five levels envisaged by the new British system are usually presented as levels through which one can progress, the level at which one enters the qualification system depends crucially on educational status — or, still, at the lower levels, on whether one was deemed bright enough — at the now-or-never age of 17 — to be selected for a craft or technician apprenticeship.

So, the two systems are similar in the way they provide a pay hierarchy in which the majority of those in the labour market — those who do not proceed to higher education — are expected to 'find their place' at an early stage in life — as high school leaver, middle school leaver in Japan, as technician, craftsman, semi-skilled or unskilled worker in Britain. But whereas qualifications are the legitimating criterion for this division in Britain (not only the criterion for pay, but also a necessary legitimator of workplace authority) this is not the case in Japan where qualifications are recognized, if at all, only in marginal bonus adjustments or somewhat faster promotion up a seniority scale. This allows the Japanese system to be functional and flexible. It subjects the British system to powerful pressures towards rigidity and preoccupation with hierarchy and the tidying up of levels.

The contrast with Japan helps to show where those pressures come from, and helps consequently to resist them — if functionality and flexibility are, indeed, deemed virtues.

SALIENT FEATURES

It may be helpful to summarize some of the characteristics of the Japanese system:

The state is heavily involved in the qualification business. Its declared interest is not only — as everywhere — public safety, but also national efficiency.

Professional associations and educational institutions have far less control over the qualifying process than in most other industrial societies.

A very small expenditure by the state in maintaining a very extensive testing apparatus evokes a very great deal of learning at the monetary and effort expense of individuals and of their employers.

This effort is primarily directed towards improving the individual's capacity to do a job he is doing, or about to do, anyway, rather than improving his chance of getting a job.

Qualifications function much more as a means of raising competence levels and contributing to the individual's advancement in the enterprise in which he is employed than as a means of certifying employability in the external labour market.

Pay scales being generally linked to general educational levels and not to discrete occupational qualifications, the temptation to inflate qualification levels for status purposes is muted, and the need to tailor them — dysfunctionally — to the exigencies of pay and authority hierarchies is modified.

8

The cost of VET and how it is shared

(Note: Price translations are made at the rate: £1 = ¥220.)
Various indications of the costs of vocational education and training
— to public authorities, to individuals and households, to employers
— have been given in previous chapters. It may be useful to draw
some of these threads together and to give some overall indication
of the way costs are divided.

THE MINISTRY OF EDUCATION SYSTEM

Let us look first at the educational institutions within the purview of
the Ministry of Education — that is to say the regular schools and
universities and the special training schools which are not under the
jurisdiction of another ministry. They constitute nearly but not quite
the whole of the extra-enterprise formal system. The Ministry
calculates that the total expenditure on the activities of these schools
amounted to ¥16,944bn in 1983. This includes expenditures by the
schools from public funds, fees and donations, and expenditures by
parents on incidental expenses like school outings, textbooks and
stationery and perhaps also school lunches. The sum amounts to 6.9
per cent of national income (Mombusho 1986).

Just over a half of that expenditure goes on compulsory (6 to 15)
education, just under a fifth on high schools and just over a fifth on
universities. Kindergarten took nearly four per cent, and all the rest
— the after-hours cram-schools, the Special Training Schools, etc.
— about three per cent.

The proportion of that expenditure coming from public sources
overall is estimated to be 81 per cent, with households contributing
15 per cent in fees and 4 per cent in other expenditure. The public

contribution is greatest for the primary and middle school segment (98.5 per cent) and least for the special training schools (2.7 per cent). Universities (53.5 per cent) and high schools (81.6 per cent) come in between, though it has to be remembered that the failure of the state to provide free high school education for all is a leading political issue, and it would be very surprising indeed if the published statistics did not minimise private contributions at this level in particular.

In per-pupil terms, this means that of the ¥0.513m spent per 6–15 year-old in a school year, the state and local authorities provided ¥0.506m (approx. £2,300) and of the ¥1.690m spent on each college and university student, public expenditure covers 0.904m (approx. £4,110). This less-than-2:1 ratio of public expenditure on university students to that on school children compares with something like a 6:1 ratio in Britain. British student grants are a major reason for this, of course, but it also reflects differences in relative pay of primary school teachers and university lecturers. As was pointed out in Chapter 1, at the beginning of their career, at least, primary school teachers are paid more.

THE VOCATIONAL ELEMENT

What proportion of this expenditure is on specifically vocational education? At the high school level, it is impossible to say from the published expenditure figures. (And perhaps deliberately so, according to one official. There might be complaints if the least popular education were shown to be the most expensive.) What does seem clear is that vocational courses are indeed somewhat more expensive than general courses. There is the special subsidy for equipment in vocational schools which works out at about £24 p.a. per pupil — a little under one per cent of the average per-pupil expenditure in high schools as a whole. Then there is a special vocational education allowance paid to teachers of vocational subjects and amounting to between 6 and 10 per cent of basic salary. Vocational schools must also be more expensive in consumables, and per-pupil salary budgets must be much greater in the under-subscribed agricultural high schools. Overall, however, the premium paid to the vocational streams is not likely to be much more than 7–8 per cent.

At the university level there are some not very adequate figures available from the triennial School Expenditure Survey. According to the most recent survey (Keihi 1984), about 65 per cent of the current expenditure in national and local government universities which can be

attributed to specific departments was spent on vocational courses —
including in the latter general science courses which cannot be properly
disentangled from engineering. Since these departments had 60 per
cent of the students, there is a tendency for vocational education to
be more expensive, as one would expect, but not a very marked one.
The differential is likely to be greater for capital expenditure.

In the case of state subsidy to the private universities, however,
the bias is stronger and clearer, partly because of explicit rules which
allow a higher level of subsidisation of salaries in medical and science
departments (Yosan 1986). In fiscal 1984, 65 per cent of the depart-
mentally attributable subsidy went to vocational courses which had
only 38 per cent of the pupils.

PUBLIC SUPPORT TO INDIVIDUALS

There is no specific programme of support for vocational education,
but there are student aid programmes for all types of education under-
taken by the Japan Scholarship Foundation (financed out of the
Ministry of Education budget). There are also schemes run by prefectural and local governments and by non-profit foundations, but they
are dwarfed in importance by the Ministry's fund which, however,
spends only about 0.3 per cent of the total higher education expenditure, public and private, and is shown by student surveys to account
for about 2.2 per cent of the average student's income (Mombu-tokei
1986, p. 150).

The scholarships — or, rather, interest-free loans — are awarded
to individual students by universities on the basis of parental income,
but the allocation to universities is intended to support the more able
students (by giving larger allocations to the more prestigious universities with difficult entrance examinations) and also those on vocational
courses. Thus, over a third of the students at teacher training colleges,
and nearly a quarter of those at colleges of technology receive grants
compared with an overall percentage of about 18 per cent.

HOUSEHOLD EXPENDITURE

The contribution of households to the education of their children is
considerable. The estimate worked out from family budget surveys
puts it at about one-fifth of total expenditure on education, or 1.3 per
cent of GNP. The survey (of wage and salary-earners' families; for the

family enterpriser fifth of the population, the figures may well be higher) shows the average household with a househead aged 30–34 spending £25 a month on education, a figure which rises to its peak — over £90 in recent years — when the househead is in his late 40s (Katsuyo 1984).

Kindergarten is the first large expenditure. Fees average a little over £600 per annum in 1985, and are not a great deal higher for the very small percentage of children in private primary and middle schools — just under and just over £1,000 respectively (Yosan 1986). Public primary and middle schools do not charge tuition fees, so that payments for PTA membership, school meals and travel expenses constitute the total household expenditure on schools — except for the out-of-school lessons at the cram-schools and other leisure interest juku which can be quite costly — about £500 a year for a primary, and £870 for a middle-school child according to a survey by the Tokai Bank (*Tokyo Shimbun*, 27 March 1986).

At the high school level, the public schools also charge fees — about £340 in 1985, compared with £930 as the average fee in private high schools. A high proportion of parents also bear the cost of sending their child to a cram school to improve their chances in the university entrance competition. These cost, on average, only a little under £1,000. In public high schools, no differences are made between general and vocational courses, though there may be extra costs for tools and materials at vocational schools — outweighed by the fact that vocational school pupils are much less likely to attend expensive cram schools.

More than half of the private expenditure on education goes on college and university fees, however — £1,200 per annum for a public four-year university and a wide range of fees for private universities — the average being £2,500 for humanities and £3,200 for science courses, though to that has to be added matriculation fees in the first year which amount to at least half of a year's tuition. And all this takes no account of student maintenance. The 1983 survey of how students cover their expenses — fees and living expenses — puts the total amount of 'subsidies received from family' at around 2,200 billion yen — about 70 per cent greater than the total amount spent on fees. (Students' own expenses from part-time work amounted to ¥510bn. 'The subsidies from family' do not count subsidies received in kind by students living at home.) (Mombu-tokei 1986)

Then there is the very considerable expenditure on special training schools for those who follow high school with a vocational course rather than college or university. Here we have some reasonably good statistics for the *senshu* category, but not for the *kakushu* 'miscellaneous school' category. The former had annual fees of 36,000 yen per annum for the public sector schools (about a tenth of the total provision), and around 800,000 yen for the private schools. With around 42,000 pupils at the former and 500,000 at the latter, that works out at around ¥400bn per annum. For the kakushu schools we must estimate. Suppose that between the kakushu fees and senshu fees, there is the same ratio as between the minimum number of annual hours they are respectively required to teach for legal recognition (680:800). Suppose, also, that a half of the kakushu students are enrolled in courses lasting one year and the other half in courses lasting three months only. That would give us (there are about 530,000 of these pupils, about 10,000 in public schools) a further household expenditure sum of ¥220bn, making a total for this type of school of ¥620bn.

OTHER EXTRA-ENTERPRISE VOCATIONAL TRAINING

Outside the purview of the Ministry of Education at least ten other ministries have within their budget funds for promoting vocational skills, either by training or by operating testing services for professional or craft qualifications. Of these the Ministry of Labour is far and away the most important — the breakdown of its ¥88bn budget is shown in Table 4.2. The other ministries' training budget amounts to around ¥3bn, and the expenditure of all ten ministries on testing totals ¥1½bn, of which the Ministry of Labour accounts for more than a half. The tests are partly self-financing from test-takers' fees. If one assumes that test-taking is as popular throughout the country as in Tokyo prefecture (the one prefecture for which Ministry of Labour test-taking figures are available) — and there *are* reasons for thinking that this would underestimate total test-taking — and assuming an average of ¥12,000 for the (variable) cost of taking the test, then the testees would contribute ¥600m to the Ministry of Labour's testing system which compares with the Ministry's ¥780m. Assuming the same ratio for the other ministries gives a figure of ¥1.2bn for testees' expenditure on tests, which, various surveys suggest, may be divided about equally between individuals and their employers.

Another item to be estimated is expenditure on correspondence courses. For the 169 courses sanctioned by the Ministry of Education there are statistics of takers. (See Chapter 6, p. 99 and Kakushu 1986, p. 88.) If one takes only the 117 courses listed as of vocational value, ignoring the doll-making and music and calligraphy courses, total expenditure by 150,000 people (the 1985 figure), at an average of 22,000 yen a course (see Kakushu 1986), would amount to three and a quarter billion yen.

The other 1,100 vocationally-useful courses on the Ministry of Labour's approved list, may not have quite as many subscribers, but on the other hand they seem on average to be a little more expensive. Total income per course ought not to be lower for these other courses since a large proportion of them are produced by commercial bodies for profit whereas the Ministry of Education's list, for which the figures were just given, is of course run by non-profit bodies. If one assumes the same expenditure per course, then we arrive at the figure of ¥35bn for total expenditure on vocational correspondence courses (£160m), which one might again assume to be equally divided between individuals and employers.

TRAINING WITHIN PRIVATE ENTERPRISE

Let us accept as a starting point the figure quoted in Chapter 6; 1,022 yen a month per employee as the average monthly expenditure on training in enterprises with more than thirty employees. And then let us assume that, given that the General Affairs Agency's Establishment Survey puts 18.8m of the 35.4m employees it enumerates (it omits government and agriculture/fisheries) in establishments with more than thirty workers, it would be reasonable to assume that of the same Agency's Labour Survey total of 42.6m employees (1984), 24m are in enterprises with more than thirty employees. And let us assume that in the smaller enterprises training expenditure is on average one-third of that in the larger ones. That would give a total of ¥370bn — in which, of course, the employers' contribution to correspondence courses and test-taking are included. As noted earlier (in the discussion of training budget: Chapter 6), this is without question an understatement since indirect staff costs, travel costs, etc. are not normally included in training budgets. Without accepting the Matsushita estimate, quoted on page 81, that true costs were four to five times the training budget, one might agree that it would be reasonable to double that figure — on the assumption that the time taken up in mutual learning and teaching in Japanese factories should be evaluated at opportunity cost rather than at salary cost — in terms of what the people involved would be doing otherwise.

TRAINING BY PUBLIC SECTOR EMPLOYERS

The public sector in Japan consists (or consisted before the current privatization programme) of public corporations and national enterprises (National Railways, Tobacco Corporation, Nippon Telegraph and Telephone etc.) as well as central and local administration. The Establishment Survey put the figure for total employees in the public sector as thus defined at 5.6m. If we assume that the per-employee training in this sector is on average similar to that in private enterprises with more than thirty employees — and, applying the same argument as in the previous paragraph, double the total to allow for indirect costs, we arrive at a figure of ¥137bn.

EMPLOYEES' 'OWN TIME' TRAINING

Although not accounted for in the national income, it would be worthwhile to evaluate the time given over by workers to after-hours study in the factory and at home, if not at overtime rates, at least at normal wage rates. Consider:

(a) The material in our earlier discussion of worker involvement and commitment (Chapter 6) as the (admittedly tenuous) basis for the guess that the average worker spends one hour a week of 'own time' on some kind of training activity. (The — possibly one million — correspondence course takers would alone make a considerable contribution to the average.)

(b) The Ministry of Labour's monthly labour statistics (1985 average) showing average monthly pay as ¥310,000 and average work hours of 176 per month; thus an average hourly pay of ¥1,766.

(c) The statistics for the employed labour force just cited.

Using the above, one arrives at an estimated contribution of ¥4,058bn and ¥493bn respectively for the private and public sectors.

A FINAL SUM

We might finally put all these figures together in a single table showing the division of costs between the three main contributors.

142

Expenditure on vocational education and training, 1984–6, by spender

Type of VET	Public sector	(¥ billion) Households	Private sector employers
Vocational high schools	910	205	
Public training schools (Ministry of Labour)	61	1	
Private special training schools	14	620	
Public training schools (Other Ministries)	90		
Vocational courses in universities			
Public (National and local)	690	72	
Private	312	580	
Sub-total, vocational education	2,077	1,478	0
Training within private enterprises			
Correspondence courses	1	18	18
Other	13	4,058	740
Training within public sector	137	493	
Skill tests/professional exams	2	1	1
Sub-total, vocational training	153	4,570	759
Totals	2,230	6,048	759

Notes

1. The cost figures for vocational high schools are taken from Mombusho 1986, and represent 35 per cent of both private and public expenditure on all high schools.

2. For public universities the Mombu-tokei 1986 figures for 1983 expenditure are used and fees substracted to give state expenditure. Both that and the fee figure are multiplied by 65 per cent to give the vocational element. For private universities, the state subsidy derives from Keihi 1984. That is subtracted from 38 per cent of total expenditure to give private expenditure on vocational education.

3. Junior colleges are omitted and post-graduate per capita costs and fees are treated as equal to those of undergraduates.

4. Colleges of Technology are treated as vocational high schools for the first three years (hence the 35 per cent figure, above) and as part of higher education for the last two years.

Anyone who has followed the arguments of the preceding paragraphs will not need telling that these figures are based on assumptions which it is conventional to call heroic, but which might be better described as foolhardy. They should be read only as providing a plausible indication of the rough orders of magnitude involved.

As the table shows, it all adds up to an expenditure on vocational education and training of around ¥9 trillion, or just below 4 per cent of the national income (about ¥240 trillion) — though only half of that sum — the half which excludes the estimate of learners' 'own time' expenditure — is actually counted in national income.

Once again, employers do not emerge as the big spenders. Their contribution works out at around ¥900bn (£4bn), well below one per cent of GNP. This compares with an estimate of £5.5bn or 1.85 per cent of GNP spent on adult and youth training by British public and private employers according to an estimate reported in the *Financial Times* (3 September 1987).

9

Policies and prospects

POLICY CO-ORDINATION

In whatever other respect Japan might be a model to us all, national policy co-ordination in the field of vocational education and training is not its strong point. MITI has a vigorous programme for training in the field of computer software writing, involving the establishment of a quango (somewhat on the lines of the energy conservation body described in Chapter 6) and the drafting of a piece of empowering legislation. Ask a senior official of the 90-person-strong bureau in charge of the Ministry of Labour's VET policy about MITI's initiative and he will give you a wry smile and tell you that *sekushonarizumu* is a major failing of the Japanese bureaucracy. Yes, he has vaguely heard of what MITI is doing, and he would expect to receive a draft of the legislation when it is complete but before it goes to the Diet. But computer skills are all MITI's side of the agreed truce lines. It would not be proper for him to make inquiries.

What this sectionalism is the price of, of course, is precisely the departmental devotion, the loyalty and identification with the department's programmes which makes the Japanese civil servant so eminently capable of taking creative and effective initiatives within his allotted sphere. Japan has been an economic growth society for so long that initiative-taking, rather than trouble-shooting or empire-building or resisting cuts, has become institutionalized as the major sphere in which the competitive energies of civil servants are mobilized. It is over proposals for new money-spending initiatives that section competes with section when the bureau is formulating its budget in early spring, over those new initiatives that bureau competes with bureau when the ministry is formulating its proposals in early summer, and over those initiatives that ministry competes with ministry in the lobbies of the Ministry of Finance — privately all through the autumn and then publicly all through the winter between the publication of the first draft and the final third draft spending plan. And for individual careers, too, it is by playing a leading role as brain-father or champion of the team's initiative — as the one who scores the goals while discreetly giving others the credit — that a good civil servant gets noticed.

Bureaucratic sectionalism tends to break down when issues are politically sensitive, so that 'the Government' has to be seen to be doing something. Then the Liberal Democratic Party begins to intervene, and the Minister may cease to be just a champion of his own civil servants and start trying to impose a policy co-ordinated at the level of the government as a whole. It is a sign of the non-controversial nature of VET that a sectionalist *modus vivendi* can reign undisturbed.

What has become controversial, of course, is the mainstream educational system. The political response — the Ad Hoc Commission on Educational Reform — was launched with great éclat as a major policy initiative of Nakasone's Prime Ministership. The main focus of concern, however, turned out to be the balance between discipline, hard work, conformity and patriotic deference on the one hand — all those qualities which have got Japan where it is — and, on the other, a more aggressive and creative individualism which some people see as necessary for Japan to get to where they would like it to be. More, or less, vocational education in the classroom was hardly an issue; the trend away from vocational and towards general courses at the high school level was hardly remarked. Nor did one hear any of the concern expressed in Anglo-Saxon societies about the efficiency of the schools in delivering basic numeracy and literacy.

Lifelong education — how, given the accelerating rapidity of technological change, to provide for continuous knowledge upgrading — *was* an issue, if a minor one. The major result in this direction was an effort to push the various ministries which run skill tests towards greater 'open access' — the lowering or abolition of entry qualifications mentioned in Chapter 7. There have been no calls for central coordination of VET policy, and such calls were in any case unlikely given that each Ministry had its own officials on the secretariat and often one or two 'loyal' members (usually university members who have all the research facilities of 'their' Ministry at their disposal in return for their loyalty) on the Commission itself.

There was something of a public concern with VET in the late 1950s and early 1960s when the economy began to take off and employers began to complain of shortages of skilled labour — especially those in the small-firm sector who could not afford expensive initial training and who had to pay premium starting wages to attract even the 'left-over' school-leavers after the big firms had taken their pick. That was the time when American economists' discovery of the economics of education and the 'residuals' as the secret of economic growth coloured the speeches of that most economistic of post-war Prime Ministers, Hayato Ikeda. 'Human resources' (*jinteki shigen*) were two of his favourite words.

The legal framework for the Ministry of Labour's training and testing activities — the 1959 law — was set at that time. Retraining needs from the run-down of the coal industry as cheap oil began to flow in the 1960s provided another momentary focusing of political interest (and the brilliant idea of earmarking a tiny oil-import tax for that retraining led to a valuable source of finance for vocational training as a whole, via the Employment Projects Promotion Agency). In the 1970s, the switch to slower growth after the oil shock coming, together with the realization of how much more rapidly the Japanese population's average age would rise than any other nation's before, brought the question of retraining for the older, especially the 'voluntary retired', worker into political focus — and the revision of the Vocational Training Law in 1978 was in part a response to that.

That issue still smoulders, but by and large VET is still not a matter of great political interest as it is in some other countries. No-one would think of appointing a political overlord to co-ordinate policy. Japan has so far avoided large-scale youth unemployment. If there is a concentration of unemployment among the least skilled segments of the working population, it has hitherto gone unremarked. Skill shortages are sometimes forecast — as when a MITI committee forecast a 600,000 deficit in software technicians by 1990 — but these rate only relatively restricted coverage in the industrial press. The 1984 revision of the vocational training law (the Law to Promote the Development of Vocational Skills) requires the Minister of Labour to promulgate a national plan, but this formality amounts to little more than a description of the Ministry's current budget initiatives and a forecasting of future ones. (See Cantor 1984, McDerment, RDIVT, etc. for accounts of the formal system.)

CONSULTATION AND RESEARCH

The viability of the sectionalist *modus vivendi* means that it is left to each Ministry separately to find ways of keeping in touch with its constituency, and of canvassing for suggestions about, or monitoring the effects of, its policies. The Ministry of Labour has a Central Consultative Committee (distinct from the Central Skill Development Association which has the executive function of running the testing services) on which sit eight 'men of learning and experience' (six professors, one essayist and one pension fund president), six trade unionists and six employers' representatives. The Ministry of Education has a similar Consultative Committee for Scientific and Vocational Education — similarly composed except that it does not have the formal trade union representation. Various bureaus in MITI set up ad hoc committees for separate fields — like the one quoted above on software skills, while the Enterprise Behaviour Section of the Policy Bureau, which has a watching brief for training matters in general keeps in touch with panels of outside experts and mobilizes them for particular research and consultative exercises. A similar section in MITI's Small and Medium Enterprise Agency has a similar function. The purely consultative status of the formal bodies, and the general tradition that they should allow their secretariats to set their agendas, mean that their influence on policy is not great.

Research efforts are equally multi-sourced. The Ministry of Labour has two research centres under its budgetary control — the one at its university-level Research and Development Institute of Vocational Training, and the other, a free-standing quango which takes the English title: National Institute of Employment and Vocational Research. The former is the only centre of note for work on the pedagogy of skill training, but both are engaged in socio-economic research. In the latter they are matched by the Ministry of Education's National Institute for Educational Research and by a research institute — the Japan Efficiency Association — at Sanno College which is supported by MITI. (NIER tends to stick to work related to the schools within the Ministry of Education's purview, and the JEA to research within industry, but there is a good deal of overlap.) There is also an employers' training association (the Japan Industrial and Vocational Training Association, associated with the Japan Productivity Council) which spends a little over one per cent of its half-billion yen (£2.5m) budget on research.

Both the great degree of overlap in these research activities and their overall quality may be gauged from such of it as has been cited in these pages. Very little of it is observational or interview research; the vast bulk is postal survey research with low response rates, which raises as many questions as it answers. Nevertheless, it does answer some questions and raising others is also a very useful activity. It also has to be said that Japanese policy-makers are very well-served by the established statistical services — the triennial establishment census, the annual wages survey, the monthly and annual labour surveys, the non-wage labour costs survey, etc. — which are maintained at a high standard.

RECENT TRENDS

Precisely because vocational training is not a particularly live issue — neither a political issue nor a policy issue — it is difficult to see clear trends of direction in the welter of material which fills the four main monthly magazines devoted to vocational training. However, the current consensus about directions does seem to contain the following elements.

Two areas of training which are often spoken of as problem areas where a lot more effort is needed are (a) retraining for the middle-aged with obsolete skills, particularly retraining within the company, and (b) internationalization — which means teaching managers, especially those going out to manage the production facilities which the revalued yen is driving overseas, how to speak English and how to adapt to foreign cultures.

But the emphasis on mid-life retraining is a good deal wider than concern simply for the craftsman with redundant skills. The acceleration of technical change in general and the microelectronics revolution in particular have shifted emphasis from initial to mid-career training. (This has been the more marked in Ministry of Labour circles because it failed to adapt the initial training programmes of its Vocational Training Centres to the rapid attenuation of the 15-year-old school-leaving group in the 1960s, lost out to the Special Training Schools and has never recaptured its position in the initial training field.)

One consequence is a certain shift in what one might call the ideology of training, as the modal industrial trainee is increasingly thought of as middle-class and middle-aged, rather than a rude mechanical apprentice who needs a good dose of discipline in his instruction. This is interestingly reflected in nomenclature. Prime Minister Ikeda's discovery of 'human resources' in the 1960s was mentioned earlier. The word has since fallen into disuse — a success, probably, for the left which fostered a dislike for its manipulative overtones — though the English word still figures largely in English-language handouts of Japanese companies and official bodies. Equally out of keeping with the spirit of the times is the old word *shokugyo-kunren* — 'vocational training'. It used to be the title of the Ministry of Labour's Bureau, and also of the 1959 law and the 1978 amended law. But clearly the overtones of disciplined slog are not consonant with the modern age. The word has since given way, both in the title of the Bureau and of the 1984 law, to 'vocational ability (skill) development' (*shokugyo noryoku kaihatsu*) — with its more positive, learner-participative, overtones. As such it is consonant with the other vogue word for autodidactic efforts, found especially in company training programmes — *jiko-keihatsu*, meaning something like 'self-enlightenment'.

The emphasis on self-study probably represents a good deal more than an ideological shift. It is also a response to the increasing difficulty of standard-packaging of industrial training as the skills required increasingly involve know-how arising from rapid technological developments or enterprise-specific know-how in production processing (RH 1985, p. 221). A response to this situation was chiefly sought in the 1984 overall revision of the vocational training law, and is reflected in the Ministry's budget shown in Table 6.4 — the shift in emphasis towards advisory support for, and subsidization of, enterprise training efforts, enterprise standard-setting and enterprise skill-testing to supplement the Ministry's own skill-testing system.

This emphasis on 'self-enlightenment' also reflects another trend, namely an increasing acceptance that the lifetime employment system, having survived the no-growth crisis in the mid-1970s and the adjustment to slow-growth since, is here to stay. That is to say, in spite of some marginal signs to the contrary such as the increased mobility of R & D personnel in large companies, the most complex and hard-to-learn skills (particularly those on which the competitiveness of the Japanese economy depends) will continue to be the property of the core of permanent-workers in large firms. Indeed, some people argue that such a trend towards employing highly trained core workers is increasingly becoming apparent in older and hitherto more mobile industrial societies like Britain.

And that means that mid-career upgrading, topping-up and retraining, and even initial training, have to take place in the enterprise rather than out in the market — or not at all.

Bibliography

Amano, I. (1984) 'Daigaku-gun no hikaku-bunseki' (Comparative analysis of university groupings') in T. Keii, ed. *Daigaku hyōka no kenkyū (The evaluation of universities)*. Tokyo: Todai Shuppan.

Bhasanavich, D. (1985) 'An American in Tokyo: Jumping to the Japanese beat'. *IEEE Spectrum*, September.

Cantor, L. (1984) 'The Institute of Vocational Training, Japan'. *BACIE Journal* 39, vi, 211–3.

—— (1985) 'Vocational education and training: The Japanese approach', *Comparative Education* 21, i.

Chingin (1984) Rodosho Seisaku-chosabu (Ministry of Labour, Policy Research Divn.), *1984 Chingin rōdōjikan seido-to sōgō chōsa hōkoku (Comprehensive survey of wages, work hours, etc.)*

Chung, P.S. (1986) 'Engineering education systems in Japanese universities', *Comparative Education Review* 30, iii, August.

Dore, R.P. (1981) *Energy conservation in Japanese industry*, London: PSI.

—— (1986) 'Where will the Japanese Nobel prizes come from?', *Science and Public Policy*, 13, vi, December.

Grayson, L.P. (1983a) 'Leadership or stagnation? A role for technology in mathematics, science and engineering education', *Engineering Education*, February.

—— (1983b) 'Japan's intellectual challenge: The strategy', *Engineering Education*, December.

—— (1984a) 'Japan's intellectual challenge: The system', *Engineering Education*, January.

—— (1984b) 'Japan's intellectual challenge: The future', *Engineering Education*, February.

Haiteku (1986) Koyo Sokushin Jigyodan, Shokugyo kunren kenkyu sentaa (Vocational Training Research Centre, Employment Promotion Agency), *Haiteku-jidai no chiiki shinko to hitozukuri (Regional development and person development in the age of high technology)*, Tokyo.

Hata, M. (1975–6) 'Shingaku-ritsu o shihyō to shita Kōtō gakkō kakusa no bunseki' ('Analysis of differences between high schools as measured by university progression rates'), *Nagoya Daigaku Kyōikugakubu Kiyo*, Vols 22, 23.

Hayes, C., Fonda, N. and Anderson, A. (1984) *Competence and Competition*, NEDO/MSC.

Hirono, R. and Asanuma, K. (1983) 'Industrial skills and training in construction industry in Japan and the UK', *Seikei-daigaku Keizaigakubu Ronshū*, 14, i, October.

Ichikawa, S. (1986) *Financial aspects of higher education in Japan*, Tokyo: National Institute for Educational Research.

IFF (1985) International Facts and Forecasting Research Ltd (for the MSC) *Adult Training Survey*.

Ishikawa, T. (1987) *Vocational Training*, Japanese Industrial Relations Series No. 7, Tokyo: The Japan Institute of Labour.

Iwaki, H. and Mimizuka, H. (1986) *Senshū, kakushu gakkō nyugakusha zō ka mekanizumu no kōkō-kaiso-betsu bunseki* (*Analysis of entrants to senshu and kakushu schools by type of high school of origin*), Tokyo: National Institute of Education (Bulletin 112).

Jiko-keihatsu (1986) Chuo Shokugyo Noryoku Kaihatsu Kyokai (National Association for the Development of Vocational Skills), *Jiko-keihatsu no tame no kunren sōgō-gaido* (*A comprehensive guide to self-development facilities*), Tokyo.

Kakushu (1986) Jiyu Kokuminsha, *Kakushu tsūshin kyoiku gaido 1987* (*1987 Guide to correspondence courses*), Tokyo. Annual.

Katsuyo (1984) Niho Seisansei Hombu (Japan Productivity Centre), *Katsuyō rōdō tokei: chingin kōshō no shihyō* (*Labour statistics for instant use: indices for wage bargainers*), Tokyo.

Keihi (1984) Mombusho (Ministry of Education), *Gakko keihi chosa* (*School expenditure survey*), Tokyo.

Keikin (1986a) Keikinzoku Yosetsu Kozo Kyokai (The Light Metals Welded Structures Association), *1986 nendo no jigyō* (*Annual action plan, 1986*), Tokyo.

—— (1986b) Keikinzoku Yosetsu Kozo Kyokai (The Light Metals Welded Structures Association), *Shōwa 60-nendo jigyō hokokusho* (*Report on activities in 1985*), Tokyo.

Kigyo (1986) '59-nendo jisseki, 60-nendo yosan ni miru kyōiku kunren-hiyo no jittai' ('The actual state of training expenditure as seen in 1985 budgets and 1984 out-turns'), *Kigyō to jinzai*, p. 19, p. 431, January.

Kinmouth, E.H. (1986) 'Engineering education and its rewards', *Comparative Education Review*, 30, iii, August.

Kokka, (1982, 1986) Jiyu Kokuminsha, *Kokka-shiken, shikaku-shiken zensho* (*Guide to state examinations and qualifying examinations*), Tokyo, annual.

Kokumin Seikatsu (1986) Kokumin Seikatsu Sentaa (National Livelihood Centre), *Kinrōsha no yoka ni kansuru chōsa*, Tokyo.

Kume, K. (1978) *Beio Kairan Jikki* (*Record of a journey to the US and Europe*), Tokyo: Iwanami.

Lorriman, J. (1986) 'Ichiban — The Japanese approach to engineering education', *Electronics and Power*, August.

McCormick, K. (1985) *Does Japan produce better engineers?*, UNCRIR. Sussex University, mimeo.

—— (1986) *New technological and organisational developments and strategies of human resource development*, UNCRIC. University of Sussex, mimeo.

McDerment, W.G. (1985) *New Technologies, education and vocational training in Japan*, Berlin: CEDEFOP.

Minkan (1986) Rodosho, Shokugyo-noryoku-kaihatsu-kyoku (Ministry of Labour, Skill Development Bureau), *Minkan kyōiku kunren jittai chōsa hōkokusho* (*Report of a survey of educational and training activities in private firms*), Tokyo.

Mombusho (1986) *Education in Japan: A brief outline*, Tokyo, Ministry of Education.

Mombu-tokei (1986) Mombusho (Ministry of Education), *Mombu tōkei yōran* (*Summary of statistics on education*), Tokyo.

ND (1986) 'Waga sha no shanai gino kentei' ('Our internal skill-test system') *Shokugyō kaihatsu jaanaru*, February.

NK (1985) Zen-Nihon Noritsu-remmei, *Kigyō-nai kyōiku ni kansuru chōsa kenkyū hōkoku: Shōwa 59-nendo chōsa hōkokusho* (*Survey on enterprise training, 1984*).

—— (1986) Zen-Nihon Noritsu-remmei, *Kigyō-nai kyōiku ni kansuru chosa kenkyu hōkoku: Shōwa 60-nendo chosa hōkokusho* (*Survey on enterprise training, 1985*).

Prais, S. (1987) 'Education for productivity: comparisons of Japanese and English schooling and vocational preparation', *National Institute Economic Review*, February.

Rawle, P.R. (1983) *The training and education of engineers in Japan*, London Business School, mimeo.

RDIVT (1984) Employment Promotion Projects Corporation, Research and Development Institute of Vocational Training, *Country Report on the planning, programming and evaluation of vocational training in Japan*, December.

Recruit (1985) *Senshū-gakkō-sei no seikatsu to ishiki* (*Life-style and opinions of senshu school students*), Tokyo Rekuruto-sha.

RH (1985) Rodosho, *Shōwa-60-nen Rōdō Hakusho* (*1985 Labour White Paper*), Tokyo: Nihon Rodo Kyokai.

Rohlen T. (1974) *For harmony and strength: Japanese white-collar organisation in anthropological perspective*, Berkeley: University of California Press.

—— (1984) *Japan's High Schools*, Berkeley: University of California Press.

Senshū (1986) Zenkoku senshu, kakushu gakko annai, Showa-62-nen (*1987 National guide to senshu and kakushu schools*) Tokyo: Obunsha.

Tsukahara, S. and Muto, H. (1986) *Development of scientific and technical manpower: The case of Japan*: Japan: National Institute of Education.

White, M. and Trevor, M. (1983) *Under Japanese management: The experience of British workers*, London: Heinemann.

Yosan (1986) Mombusho, Daijin Kambo (Ministry of Education, Science and Culture, Minister's Secretariat). *Showa-61-nendo kuni to chiho no bunka-yosan* (*Budgeted expenditure on education and culture, national and local, 1986*)

Yosetsu (1986a) Nihon Yosetsu Kyokai (The Japan Welding Engineering Society), *Go-annai* (*A Guide to the Society*), Tokyo.

—— (1986b) Nihon Yosetsu Kyokai (The Japan Welding Engineering Society), *Shikaku-nintei-seido no go-annai* (*An outline of licensed qualifications offered by the Society*).

Index

ability labelling, 14, 29
ability-distribution, between
    university courses 26-7
academic bias, xii, 14, 29;
    conservatism, 49;
    independence, xii
achievement, 10
Ad Hoc Commission on
    Educational Reform, 6, 120,
    132, 146
agriculture, 22, 33, 35; in
    universities, 47
alienation, 7
aristocratic traditions, 13
arts/science division, 28
aspirations, 24
assessment, in universities, 51;
    in vocational high schools, 42

basic research, 54
basic science, 53
below-average, education of, xii
benevolence, 90
Berg, I., 83
biotechnology, 74
boy-scout-badge approach, xiv
Britain, see UK
business courses, in high
    schools, 34, 41
business studies, in
    universities, 48

Cantor, L., 60
career structure, 3
central control, 49
central government, qualification
    examinations, 120ff
Central Skill Development
    Association, 148
certificates, see qualifications
certification, see skill tests
chair system, 49
child-centred curricula, 36
class size, 5
co-education, 20, 22
co-education, see also gender
College for Industrial Efficiency,
    97, 99, 148
College of Technology, 1, 22, 45

co-operativeness, 43
commerce, 33
commercial training, 71
competitiveness, xv; see also
    national efficiency
computer education, 44, 72
computer training, 61
computers, at schools, 5
Confucian traditions, 4, 5, 128
continuing education, see lifelong
    education
control over education, xii
core curriculum, xv
correspondence courses, xiii, 10,
    34, 68, 94-100; costs, 140-1
cost effectiveness, of public
    expenditure, 13
costs, of enterprise training, 141;
    of 'own time' training, 142; of
    VET, 136ff; of VET in public
    sector, 142; of correspondence
    courses, 98, 103, 143; of
    education to households,
    138-40; of enterprise training,
    143; of enterprise-operated skill
    tests, 105-6; of general
    education, 1; of public
    training schools, 143; of skill
    tests, 128, 143; of special
    training schools, 143; of
    vocational education, 137-8,
    143; of vocational high
    schools, 143
craftsmen, 45
cram schools, 4, 28; costs of,
    139
creativity, 11, 54
cultural factors in VET, xi

data processing, 22, 71
discipline, in schools, 6
distance learning, see
    correspondence courses, xiii
double-schooling, 72

earnings differentials, by educa-
    tional level, 31; by firm size,
    31, 110; by qualification, 106
economics, 28